South of Our Selves

South of Our Selves

Mexico in the Poems of Williams, Kerouac, Corso, Ginsberg, Levertov and Hayden

GLENN SHELDON

McFarland & Company, Inc., Publishers
Jefferson, North Carolina, and London

"The Desert Music" (excerpts) by William Carlos Williams, from *The Collected Poems of William Carlos Williams, Volume II: 1939–1962*, copyright ©1953 by William Carlos Williams. Used by permission of New Directions Publishing Corporation.

Excerpts from *Mexico City Blues* reprinted by permission of Sterling Lord Literistic Inc. Copyright 1959 by Jack Kerouac.

Gregory Corso's poems (excerpts) from the book *Mindfield: New and Selected Poems* by Gregory Corso. Copyright ©1989 by Gregory Corso. Appears by permission of the publisher, Thunder's Mouth Press.

Excerpts from "Siesta in Xbalba" from *Collected Poems 1947–1980* by Allen Ginsberg. Copyright ©1954 by Allen Ginsberg. Reprinted by permission of HarperCollins Publishers Inc. United Kingdom and British Commonwealth. Reprinted by permission of Penguin Books Ltd.

"Overland to the Islands" (excerpt), "Central Park, Winter, after Sunset" (excerpt), "Tomatlan (Variations)," (excerpt) "A Supermarket in Guadalajara" (excerpt), "Scenes from the Life of the Peppertrees" (excerpts), "Triple Feature" (excerpts), and "Xochipilli" by Denise Levertov from *Collected Earlier Poems 1940–1960*, copyright ©1957, 1958, 1959, 1960, 1961, 1979 by Denise Levertov. Used by permission of New Directions Publishing Corporation.

Excerpts from "An Inference of Mexico," from *Collected Poems of Robert Hayden* by Robert Hayden, edited by Frederick Glaysher. Copyright ©1985 by Emma Hayden. Used by permission of Liveright Publishing Corporation.

LIBRARY OF CONGRESS CATALOGUING-IN-PUBLICATION DATA

Sheldon, Glenn.
   South of our selves : Mexico in the poems of
Williams, Kerouac, Corso, Ginsberg, Levertov and Hayden /
Glenn Sheldon.
     p.   cm.
   Includes bibliographical references and index.

   ISBN 0-7864-1746-3 (softcover : 50# alkaline paper)

   1. American poetry — 20th century — History and criticism.
2. Mexico — In literature. 3. Americans — Mexico — History —
20th century. 4. Poets, American — Homes and haunts —
Mexico. 5. Mexico — Foreign public opinion, American.
6. American poetry — Mexican influences. I. Title.
PS159.M6S67   2004
811'.5093272 — dc22   2004000956

British Library cataloguing data are available

©2004 Glenn Sheldon. All rights reserved

No part of this book may be reproduced or transmitted in any form or by any means, electronic or mechanical, including photocopying or recording, or by any information storage and retrieval system, without permission in writing from the publisher.

Manufactured in the United States of America

Cover photograph ©2004 ClipArt.com

McFarland & Company, Inc., Publishers
  Box 611, Jefferson, North Carolina 28640
    www.mcfarlandpub.com

To Rane,
who read, reread, critiqued and recritiqued
this work selflessly and patiently

Acknowledgments

An earlier version of a portion of Chapter 1 appeared in *The Journal of Imagism* as "Poet on a Transnational Bridge: William Carlos Williams's Identity Politics in 'The Desert Music.'" Author retains rights.

An earlier version of another portion of Chapter 1 appeared in *The CEA Critic* as "William Carlos Williams's Babel of Voices in the Long Poem 'The Desert Music.'" The author is grateful to CEA Publications for permission to reprint this material.

An earlier version of Chapter 3 appeared in *The McNeese Review* as "Gregory Corso: Writing Back Home from Mexico." The author thanks *The McNeese Review* for permission to reprint this material.

Table of Contents

Acknowledgments vii
Introduction: New Maps for Old Maps 1

1. WILLIAM CARLOS WILLIAMS 13
2. JACK KEROUAC 31
3. GREGORY CORSO 67
4. ALLEN GINSBERG 91
5. DENISE LEVERTOV 123
6. ROBERT HAYDEN 147
7. CONCLUSION 175

Works Cited 179
Index 187

Introduction:
New Maps for Old Maps

This study focuses on specific American poetry from the 1950s. Particularly, I look at poems by several American poets who visited Mexico in the 1950s and wrote poems based on those experiences. By traveling "south of the border," what may we learn about our selves? Keeping in mind that the "tourist gaze is intrinsically part of contemporary experience" and that "people are much of the time 'tourists' whether they like it or not" (Urry 74), I was intrigued by how such experiences play out in poetic texts that involve travel at the mid-century mark. Most of the works in this study fit neatly in the following categories: long poems, poem sequences or — in the case of Jack Kerouac — an entire poetry collection. The experiences recorded are varied and intriguing, from some mere snapshots or postcard-like vignettes to in-depth aesthetic and journalistic inquiries.

Rather than the contemporary experience of gazing upon "ideal representations of the view in question that [we] internalize from postcards and guidebooks (and TV programmes and the internet)" (Urry 78), I focus on real (if literary) representations of the view, specifically Mexico from the perspectives of U.S. poets. Specific works which I use for my project include William Carlos Williams's long poem "The Desert Music"; Jack Kerouac's poetry book *Mexico City Blues*, primarily the "12th Chorus," "116th Chorus," "134th Chorus" and the "222nd Chorus"; Gregory Corso's poem sequence "Mexican Impressions" and the short poem "Puma in Chapultepec Zoo"; Allen Ginsberg's long poem "Siesta in Xbalba"; Denise Levertov's poem sequence "Tomatlan (Variations)," "Overland to the Islands," "A Supermarket in Guadalajara, Mexico," the poem sequence "Scenes from the Life of the Peppertrees," "Triple Feature" and, finally, "Xochipilli"; and Robert Hayden's poem sequence "An Inference of Mexico."

This book, in part, flushes out literary issues of Americanness. The poems I've selected foreground the complex, and sometimes contradictory, relationships between and among the following: location, writing, society, history, re-vision and dislocation. My selections address the complexities of the United States and its identity (identities) at the mid-century interstice. The spaces from which these writers speak and write indeed examine notions of provincial space (the United States) and cosmopolitan space, as well as local, regional and global identities, keeping in mind that by "provincial" I do not intend to imply urban superiority over rural life, as it is frequently used. I use it as a term for a restricted, or myopic, view or intellectual outlook, particularly as it relates to global culture and notions of universality.

The poems examined here reveal interesting links among the writers, along with important differences that are sometimes directly attributable to issues of class, race, sexual orientation and gender. As these poets experience their versions of Mexico, ironically, questions about the American writer move into the foreground. In *The Tourist Gaze*, John Urry reminds us that when we travel "we look at the environment with interest and curiosity. It speaks to us in ways we appreciate, or at least we anticipate that it will do so" (1). Not only do we "look at the environment," but we inevitably compare and contrast our experiences with our sense of "home" and "self," two important topics of American identity, that are influenced by both the internalization of the greater American society and the redefinition of citizenship in an increasingly global world. This study offers a look at how these pressures surface within literary texts.

Overall, this project outlines the relationships, direct or indirect, of poets visiting Mexico and writing poems that grapple with issues of the self and others, issues that become prominent because of geographical and cultural dislocations. The chapters following the introduction are not arranged in the order in which the poems were written or published; however, they are not ordered arbitrarily because each chapter further advances notions of locality toward the universal, the inclusive or both.

The work as it unfolds over the next several chapters addresses notions and issues dealing with "Americanness," by which I mean the United States as presented by the poets here. When I use the term North America, I intend the continent, which, of course, includes Mexico. I do recognize that the terms "America" and "Americanness" are problematic; it has been our critical tradition to call the United States "America," and things and people within it "American." I am interested in how we negotiate such terms. Placement and displacement reveal as much of a culture's psychic geography as of its physical geography.

One Spanish adjective for things and people from the U.S. is *estadounidense,* which can be translated literally as "United Stateser" or "from the United States"; however, this apt term sounds excessively clunky in English. Until a more accurate term gains usage, I stay with the terms America and American — with all due apologies for the ethnocentrism those words imply and, perhaps, reinforce. The chapter on William Carlos Williams, Chapter 1, introduces key concepts surrounding these ideas, allowing each subsequent chapter to further investigate these initial ideas.

Inherent in the concept of Americanness is, of course, notions of the "foreign" or "foreignness," which is significantly tied to notions of "home" as well. Frequently defined by political, national and cultural borders, the space of the foreign is, generally speaking, a location where an individual feels like a visitor, a guest or, perhaps, an individual in unsafe territory, be it physical or cultural. Typically, I use the word foreign as a notion of location where the territory and culture(s) are, somehow, distinct from one's own. Often this is defined by what is unfamiliar and undesirable to a majority; the positionality of a speaker or writer obviously shapes the final version of the experience — whether that experience be known, unknown or new.

Home can be defined by location as much as by dislocation (as in the sense of foreign space). I use "home" conceptually as one, or more, primary places — typically geographical — that an individual considers formative or congenial. Typically, this place may be where one is born, as for Jack Kerouac in Chapter 2, but it is not limited to such origins. Allen Ginsberg, in Chapter 4, identifies home as either aesthetic (San Francisco) or global. Typically, home is where one feels safe, where one is generally a comfortable "citizen" of its territory and local culture(s), which can be seen clearly in Chapter 3 where Gregory Corso resists Mexico as a place and as an idea. Often defined by what is familiar and desirable, rather than what is "foreign," home is sometimes — as in Corso's case — partly defined by "not here."

The key concepts that arise in this book are central to notions of Americanness, as well as to U.S. dominance, hegemony and western European imperialism of North and South American cultures (particularly indigenous cultures); thus, by looking at Mexico through the eyes of American poets, the reader is forced to reconsider the greater world, one outside of our local "borders." Mexico, as part of the "Hispanic" world (which transcends borders, including U.S. borders), helps construct the United States and its own ideas of political and cultural borders. As a term, Hispanic is fraught with controversy, derision and division. In this study, I use the word to include people and things of Spanish and Portuguese heritage in South, Central and North America, as well as the Caribbean. The term implies a history of conquest, dual and multiple identities, and the metastructure of domination from which self-naming (Latino, Chicana, Nuyorican, etc.) emerges, and it can reveal other-naming (which is frequently just plain racism).

Poems, particularly as viewed as anthropological and cultural artifacts, serve as potent tools of cultural production and reproduction. As reproduction, in the course of this study, readers may see a reification of the systems that produce culture, from high culture to mass culture, and the social and economic implications of those systems. As social and historical artifacts, the poems I include here seem to clearly reflect a time and place in American history, the 1950s, when notions of oppositional dialectics were, arguably, at their strongest. As this study "progresses"— theoretically rather than temporally — I intend to show that such notions, while dominant, were not naturalized, universal axioms, but constructions of myriad forces at work in U.S. hegemony (a philosophy or notion that underscores the system of control, imposition

Introduction

and domination of one group by another, often resulting in the erasure of profound differences).

William Carlos Williams, Jack Kerouac, Gregory Corso, Allen Ginsberg, Denise Levertov and Robert Hayden are all invested in challenging hegemony, on some level, but clearly some succeed more than others in their resistance, while one or two may seem lost or appropriated by the status quo, particularly in the case of some of the Beat authors. John Lardas astutely observes: "In challenging the legitimacy of the status quo, the Beats ironically reproduced many of the assumptions which were part of the myth of American exceptionalism" (111). The question becomes, how to avoid reproduction? One method that informs the noble work of challenging hegemony, I believe, is the inclusion of voices other than the one "owned" by the status quo, which may be one's own voice. This inclusivity, if you will, frequently permits the creative writer an opportunity to challenge the self, which perhaps "lies in the ability of the human memory to negotiate the distance between time past and time present and the capacity of a profoundly sympathetic imagination to transcend the space between self and other" (W. Williams 163). Such transcendence, particularly as it occurs through differing voices and/or multiple layers of texts, is what may be found in some or all of these poets' works.

Hopefully, one of the things we will find is a poetic "identity more universal, as a denizen of the cosmos" (Mullen 242). The poems in this project address the complexities of the United States and its identity (identities) in the mid-century mark. Caren Kaplan makes the intriguing suggestion that "[r]epresentational practices of all kinds, from ethnographies to popular films to postcards, produce views of the world that participate in discourses of displacement in powerful ways" (61). I add that such practices also participate in discourses of placement, including those defined by geography, gender and culture, as well as others.

The spaces from which these writers speak and write open up an examination of notions of space and one's own position in a culture; these notions in turn inform issues of local, regional and global identities, and perhaps some confirmation of "the oneness of mankind" (Harper 74). Here I offer new maps for old maps, readings of American poets reading another's culture. It is easier from our contemporary perspective to view the world globally and to understand the fluidity of borders and border crossings. From the decade of the 1950s, these concepts were still being explored. Mexico was still generally viewed as *south* of our selves, remote and removed from our national identity. Each poet here attempts to come to terms with his or her American self by going south of the border; in point of fact, the borders being crossed often lie within the poets themselves. Hence, these border crossings become curious but important postcards, slices of life or documentaries on our national identity at the mid-century mark.

First, in Chapter 1, I focus upon William Carlos Williams. In the fall of 1950, William Carlos Williams crossed the Texas-Mexico border into Juárez for an evening with his wife and old friend Robert McAlmon. Out of that brief visit came his important poem "The Desert Music" (1951); the 354-line, multi-voiced poem represents a genuine rebirth for his late poetic career.

William Carlos Williams's identity as one of the "most American" of modern poets is informed by his ambivalence to his Puerto Rican heritage. The America that emerges from this author's brief trip to Mexico offers an invaluable vantage point, with attendant anxieties, that leads strongly into the major issues of the following chapters. Williams's central project is writing home, creating what is "American" in the United States into modern poetry.

In Chapter 2, I turn to Jack Kerouac. In the summer of 1955, Kerouac improvised the 242 choruses of *Mexico City Blues* (published 1959). Later that summer he left to join Ginsberg and others involved in the San Francisco poetry renaissance in Berkeley, California. *Mexico City Blues* allows me a unique opportunity to focus on the poetic output of an author better known for his prose. A comparable study of Kerouac's prose about Mexico would itself prove insightful, for in "*On the Road* Kerouac calls Mexico the place where we 'will finally learn ourselves'" (McCampbell Grace 113). We will see to what extent this insight extends to his book-length blues poem sequences.

This work, *Mexico City Blues*, is the most problematic text in this study; it is extremely fluid and impressionistic in its methods of composition and interpretation. Kerouac's foray into Mexico covers the

Introduction

range of experiences: acceptance, fetishization, fear and dismissal. Kerouac's poetry collection displays a real absence of Mexico despite his extended stays; his French-Canadian heritage and "hybrid status" (McCampbell Grace 94) keeps him a "foreigner" in the United States. Feeling even more the outsider in Mexico, he attempts to write to home, to his sense of a home in the United States.

In Chapter 3, I look at Gregory Corso. In a brief trip (October–November 1956) with Ginsberg, Corso stopped in Guadalajara to see Levertov and Goodman. *Gasoline* (1958), a collection of poems, was written during this trip; significantly, Corso offers a "comic" vantage point unique among his contemporaries. The youngest member of the Beat poets, Corso sees only death in Mexico, which permeates the poem sequence "Mexican Impressions" and at least one other poem in *Gasoline*.

Corso, in Mexico, writes back home in the sense of trying to return back home; his works reify the foreignness of Mexico and center his own complex and problematic American identity and notions of the United States. Ironically, a man who has dealt with "displacement" on so many personal and social levels feels displaced by his visit to Mexico, which may serve to confirm that, at least for Corso, an "aversion to the dominant symbols of postwar American might was not an outright rejection of the 'American Way of Life'" (Lardas 178).

In Chapter 4, I turn to the most famous of the Beat poets: Allen Ginsberg. Ginsberg's poem "Siesta in Xbalba" highlights a bold, sexual and defiant side of Mexico, the American tourists and the Mexican citizens. Experience at its most heightened level is the goal for Ginsberg's literary output from Mexico or about Mexico. He offers an unabashed queer view from his own and always unique perspective.

Ginsberg is, in essence, writing for home, for a new idea of what the United States could be; his awareness of the oppositional dialectics of 1950s U.S. society leads him to a cosmic revelation in relation to U.S. culture and society. Ginsberg, for one, is ever conscious of oppositional dialectics at work, as he attempts to get beyond them and, thus, follows the urges toward a cosmic position as a poet. In the process, the local and the cosmic become negotiated through his complex American identity.

In Chapter 5, I look at several poems by Denise Levertov. She lived in Mexico from 1956 to 1958 with her American husband. In these and subsequent years Levertov wrote many poems about Mexico: "a country whose beauty haunted her" (Rodgers 67). As a British-born "Americanized" citizen (my categorization), Levertov is invaluable to this study for her methods of composition and interpretation and her connections to American poetry in the vein of Williams. Indeed, Levertov's identity is a complex one, not unlike others in this overall study; in Gary Pacernick's "Interview with Denise Levertov," she states: "I *don't* consider myself a Jewish poet. Nor do I consider myself a Welsh, English, American, New York, Massachusetts, Californian, or Seattle poet, nor a Catholic poet. I cannot be categorized except as a mish-mash" (91). Rather than labeling her a "mish-mash" throughout the course of this study, I view her — with all due apologies — as an American poet. In that respect, I am lucky, because I could find no other major American female poet who visited Mexico in the 1950s and wrote about those experiences. Without Levertov, this would be a purely masculinist study. Although Levertov cannot be held up as an example of what any female poet of the age would accomplish by visiting (or in her case, living in) Mexico, I am fortunate to have at least a glimpse of one woman's articulation of such an experience.

Lastly, Levertov's experiences, as present in her poems about Mexico, accentuate acceptance and welcome of the new, the different, rather than fearing or dismissing the foreign. Levertov is always writing at home, wherever she may be, for her sense of location is hybridized (like her identity). She says, "I have never really 'belonged' anywhere, and therefore to some degree am at home anywhere" (Pacernick 92). Wherever she may belong, what is found in her works is very important to this study and to a turning of the American "view" of Mexico, its people and its culture(s), and this may be due to being "at home anywhere."

Finally, in this study, I turn to the often under-appreciated poet Robert Hayden. Indeed, it "remains a mystery ... [that] so many of Hayden's best lyrics have received virtually no commentary at all" (Goldstein 3). Like Levertov's identity, Hayden's is more complex than simply "African American." According to W.D. Snodgrass,

Introduction

Robert Hayden's mother, a glamorous woman of mixed race, appeared to be white; his father, Asa Sheffey, was a black laborer. That marriage failed, and, at eighteen months, Robert was given to be raised by Sue Ellen and William Hayden. At that time he was rechristened; some question arose whether he had been legally adopted [223].

Hybridized as that sounds, Hayden self-identifies as an African American. And as an African-American poet, Hayden offers an interesting overview of how class, race, politics and religion serve to inform the writer. In turn, these issues force readers to renegotiate dominant discourse. His poem "An Inference of Mexico" is an excellent example of seeing beyond one's own cultural baggage, both in his utilization of "multivocal talents" (W. Williams 166) and language usage that is "bidialectic and dialectical" (Boyd 211).

Hayden, primarily, is writing homes. In "Mean to Be Free," Edward Hirsch states: "Because no single place was home for him, every place was home" (80). Hayden's sense of location is more universalized for very particular reasons; in his work, Mexico and the United States could each represent a global home. Dislocation, in his gaze, is cultural more than topographical. "Central to much tourism is some notion of departure, particularly that there are distinct contrasts between what people routinely see and experience and what is extraordinary, the extraordinary sometimes taking the form of a liminal zone" (Urry 124). Hayden's liminal zone, significantly, includes the African-American experience both at home and in Mexico. Hirsch emphasizes that "[h]owever internationalist [Hayden] was in outlook, his life's work emphasizes that he was an American poet, deeply engaged by the topography of American myth in his efforts to illuminate the American black experience" (80). This illumination informs both his poems about the United States and his poem sequence about Mexico.

Indeed, overall this project is but a threshold for further considerations of poetry and place, "Americanness" and "away," as well as a way to look at sometimes contradictory relationships between and among location, writing, society, history, re-vision and dislocation. Gloria Anzaldúa, in *Borderlands/La Frontera: The New Mestiza,* admonishes Americans or, more specifically, "gringos" to: "Admit that Mexico is your double ... [and] accept the doppelgänger in your psyche" (86). This admission is an important precursor in recognizing Mexico's presence within our own national discourses. In going south of themselves, these poets writing during the 1950s intentionally and sometimes unintentionally complicate our literary provincialism, turning away from Europe to Mexico as a source and resource for our U.S. national imaginings.

"Admit that Mexico is your double ... [and] accept the doppelgänger in your psyche"

— Gloria Anzaldúa,
*Borderlands/La Frontera:
The New Mestiza*

1

William Carlos Williams

Among the trips that the poets in this study took to Mexico, William Carlos Williams's was the shortest one; he crosses from El Paso into Juárez just for dinner. That brief experience becomes the impetus for his major, long poem "The Desert Music," a multi-voiced work about a very personal quest. Recovering from a stroke and questioning the meaning of his life, Williams, in the space of the poem, confronts Hispanic culture, as well as his own identity as half Puerto Rican.

For this "most American of poets," according to the critics, Williams investigates his Americanness and his own ambivalence about his Hispanic heritage. In other words, Mexico forces Williams to grapple with his Puerto Rican heritage, which he, generally, kept far in the background of his public literary persona.

"The Desert Music" begins on a transnational bridge between the United States and Mexico. A sleeping figure on that bridge appears to strike at the core of Williams's being, as if the sleeping figure and Williams's psyche are one. Urry reminds us that "the gaze of the tourist can be amazingly fickle, searching out or anticipating something new or something different" (10). From the moment Williams steps on to that bridge, he seems to expect "something new or something different." As "The Desert Music" continues, multiple voices and sounds fill the poem; the exterior world informs Williams's interior world and his own self-questioning. The active nature of both the multi-voicing as well as the sounds around him pulls the poet Williams (at this stage of his life a frail and aging man) back into the world of the living. The moment reaffirms Williams's sense of self; Williams's central project is writing home, writing himself back to what is "American" in the United States.

The border crossing in "The Desert Music" allows Williams enough psychic distance to consider the vastness of the American experience. As Denise Levertov observes: "Doc Williams, shrewd, practical, skeptical, as some admirers see him and as he liked to present himself (even to himself) was at the same time a poet ('I am, I am a poet'—he repeats in 'The Desert Music') with all of the archetypal poet's resemblance to the archetypal mystic" (Levertov, "Williams and the Duende" 41–42). Note how in the above passage, the notion of place is emptied out, that Williams is seen as archetypal but at the cost of the contexts in which he wrote. He may indeed be a "mystic" in the sense of his ability to meditate, a talent and skill often possessed by poets, and yet his brief dinner in Mexico is not merely an interior journey. By noting the many voices around him, many of them more sound than communication, Williams writes of home as a real place inhabited by its real citizens in all their contradictions.

Williams had never journeyed into Mexico until after World War II; "Dr. Williams spent two days in 1906 escorting a patient to San Luis Potosí but had not attempted to explore farther, a fact that seems surprising in view of his lifelong interest in Latin American culture" (Gunn 234). In 1950, Williams and his wife Flossie crossed the border "for only an evening while he and his wife visited their old friend Robert McAlmon in El Paso" (Gunn 234). That brief experience becomes the basis for the multi-voiced poem "The Desert Music" (1951), which represents a genuine rebirth for his late poetic career. It is the work of a mind whose journey is about mental distances and not physical distances. Here we must be clear that Williams is a poet, as well as a thinker. His work is greatly influenced by his theorist friend Kenneth Burke, who "denies the idea of a stable self and posits instead the idea that we are made up of a 'Babel of voices'.... Consequently, our action within history is real, though our understanding of that history is at best an imperfect interpretation of an imperfect interpretation" (Bremen 135).

1. William Carlos Williams

Williams's "The Desert Music" is indeed a departure for the famous poet, now recovering from a stroke. The poem initiates Williams's "Babel of voices"; it works as an imperfect communication of an imperfect perception of what it means to be a poet (to extend Burke's terms), as well as a self-evaluation of Williams's identity as a poet (or, more accurately, identities — as poet, doctor, Hispanic American and U.S. citizen).

"The Desert Music" is recognized by critics as quite new for Williams; indeed, it is frequently called a "cubist self-portrait" (Marzán 258). Additionally, critic Drewey Wayne Gunn praises it as "one of Williams's most important poems" (234). Gunn goes on to state that "attention to detail partly explains why the poem is one of the best written by an American about Mexico," but local color is not ultimately Williams's real concern in the poem. Rather Mexico becomes a point of isolation in which he must define the nature of poetic inspiration for himself; "William / Carlos Williams, the poet" (*l.* 235), is the poem's central character. The poet reinvents himself in a Mexico made real by his own observations and intuition; this reinvention is the poem "The Desert Music."

Interestingly, the poem begins its narrative out of sequence. The poem begins "—when the dance begins" (*l.* 1), invoking the image of a human embryonic form, apparently asleep on one of the bridges that connect Mexico with the United States. In 1963 critic Cecil Robinson saw the figure as literally a headless corpse, but every critic since then insists that the figure is merely sleeping. In "The Desert Music" Williams observes that the law would define the form as "nothing / but a corpse, wrapped in a dirty mantle" (*ll.* 39–40); however, the legality in this poem is about the law of poetry, not civil laws. For Williams, the figure on the bridge cannot be a dispensable nothing; it is, like everything to this poet, the substance for a poem.

The reader seems to arrive late at the poem, as if a performance has already begun; this form follows "the insensate music ... an agony of self-realization" (*ll.* 43–45). If the form is literally a corpse, its fetal position cannot signify eventual rebirth to Williams. After he evokes the "form," Williams immediately amplifies upon it:

>   Is it alive?
>
>   — neither a head,
>
> legs nor arms!
>
>   It isn't a sack of rags someone
>
> has abandoned here .   torpid against
>
> the flange of the supporting girder .   ?
>
>   an inhuman shapelessness,
>
> knees hugged tight up into the belly
>
>   Egg-shaped! [*ll.* 8–16]

Interestingly, Williams introduces the narrative's ultimate discovery of the figure without animating an additional verb; instead, he relies on the verb infinitive of "end":

> to end about a form
> propped motionless — on the bridge
> between Juárez and El Paso — unrecognizable
> in the semi-dark [*ll.* 1–4]

The figure, like the grammar, is suspended in potentiality. Narrative and sequence yield to the verb infinitive; they remain static until the poet, as the poem's narrator, chooses to animate such "infinities."

The shapelessness of the figure at first appears to be "inhuman" to the poem's narrator: "knees hugged tight up into the belly / Egg-shaped!" (*ll.* 15–16). The narrator is, of course, Williams himself, which the poem reveals. "So this is William / Carlos Williams, the poet" (*ll.* 272–73) states one of his Juárez dinner hosts. However, the poem is also informed by multiple voices, both exterior to the poet as well as interior to him. "The Desert Music" is indeed constructed of many voices, "as many voices as there are in a country" (Bremen 140). Paul Mariani, in his succinctly informative essay titled after the poem, praises the "poem's sharp edges and dissociated voices, its crazy quilt of forms ranging from sprawled prose to tight quatrains to heighten the 'realistic' narrative" (126). Williams is a writer who seeks to reevaluate his life in "The Desert Music." His brief visit into one of Mexico's northernmost cities becomes a physical "journey developed into explicit spiritual or mental pilgrimages" (Gunn xi), a personal journey toward transmutation, a characteristic change that suggests progress, insight and greater understanding.

Williams's mind and body become attuned to foreign surroundings; details become sources of knowledge at opportune sites for the poet. Additionally, there is a Whitmanesque cataloging throughout the poem; in the market place there are

> paper flowers *(para los santos)*
> baked red-clay utensils, daubed
> with blue, silverware,
> dried peppers, onions, print goods, children's
> clothing   [*ll.* 93–97]

The two primary "things" in the poem, however, are the bridge and the shapeless figure asleep on the bridge.

The bridge links two "sister" cities historically, as well as literally and culturally; it "spans a divided city and, symbolically at least, two cultures: Juárez, which, although an image in an English-language poem, Williams makes a point of writing with its accent, and El Paso, which although ostensibly Spanish is now English" (Marzán 243). While many critics point out that this life-affirming poem is partly a response to the despair in T.S. Eliot's *The Waste Land*, it also owes its metastructure to Hart Crane's *The Bridge*: "Williams's bridge across the Rio Grande would answer Crane's vision of hell [in *The Bridge*]" (Mariani 126). The symbol of the Indian/American muse is compacted at "the level of a burlesque queen" in both "The Desert Music" and *The Bridge* (Mariani 126). Williams's bridge, then, makes many links.

The adjectives that describe, or do not describe, the figure on the bridge in "The Desert Music" reveal that it may be not quite human. "It isn't a sack of rags" (*l.* 11) that is "torpid" and egg-shaped against "the flange of the supporting girder" (*l.* 13); yet, according to Sherman Paul, the "Indian asleep on the bridge is never as explicitly defined in the poem as he is in *The Autobiography*" (77), which is debatable. Williams writes: "Juarez, across the bridge ... tequila at five cents a glass, a quail dinner and the Mexicans, the poor Indians—one huddled into a lump against the iron-work of the bridge at night—safe perhaps from both sides, incredibly compressed into a shapeless obstruction—asleep" (388–89). This characterization is not more "explicitly defined" than the sleeping figure I find within the text of the poem. The figure or shapeless shape is introduced at the beginning of "The Desert Music" in which a "dance begins" only to "end about a form / propped motionless—on the bridge" (*ll.* 1–2).

The poem begins with a long dash, as if in interruption, but there are also the lines' movements from left to right. The first line of the poem reveals where the poem will end "about a form"; the "poem taking shape is therefore an 'interjurisdictional' dance with the embryo/form, who in the middle of the bridge on the international border is reborn in being free from rigid laws" (Marzán 245). Williams's use of relative clauses, sometimes syndetic (a relative clause frequently initiated by a conjunction), reinforces the sense of the poem itself as bridge-like. In short, the shapeless form mirrors some aspect of Williams himself

> on the International Boundary. Where else,
>
> interjurisdictional, not to be disturbed?
>
> How shall we get said what must be said?
>
> Only the poem. [*ll.* 18–21]

In the poem, the shape asleep on the bridge represents several things for Williams: it is his poetic identity, or the source of such inspiration; it is his unborn self, a sort of alter image, or doppelgänger; it is his dual identity as a Hispanic American, which has been torpid because of his own choice of making his American identity primary in his life.

The bridge, then, also functions as a metaphoric birth canal, the site for birth that fights chaos, the aridity of the desert and writer's block. "'The Desert Music' presents images by means of which the self is apprehended across the abyss of time" (Fisher-Wirth 190–91). The fetal figure on the bridge is "primal pagan ground ... the terror of birth [to Williams]" (Paul 78); however, this is a simplification of a complex moment, for the figure embodies the terror of birth, terror of death and the terror of a life without poetry.

"The Desert Music" is fertile with potential for creativity, and it is a stark view of the sense of loss that happens when the poetic self is not fulfilled. This is the dilemma that this aging, ailing poet must face within himself, when Williams confronts the figure on the bridge. The poet awakens to the potential of the desert and to the potentials buried within his Hispanic heritage. It is only on foreign soil, no matter how brief the journey, where he begins to confront the Other — defined simply here as outsidedness — inside himself. Within Williams's own Hispanic identity (as half Puerto Rican), he finds a surprising resource for creativity which becomes foregrounded in this pivotal poem.

Williams fills "The Desert Music" with Mexico's nationalistic colors — red and green: "baked red-clay utensils ... dried peppers, onions" (*ll.* 94–95), "pomegranate" (*l.* 145) and "the aniline / red and green candy" (*ll.* 150–51), as well as the "the virgin of her mind . those unearthly / greens and reds" (*ll.* 227–28). Likely, the "paper flowers *(para los santos)*" (*l.* 93) are green, white and red: the colors of Mexico's flag. Near the end of the poem, Williams describes the Mexicans, parenthetically, as "(... Indians who chase the white bastards / through the streets on their Independence Day / and try to kill them)" (*ll.* 319–21); the association of the stereotype of the "red-skinned" native is juxtaposed against the white-skinned imperialist (with its subtext of "greenbacks"). Here, conquest is a major theme in this poem, with its mention of "silverware" (*l.* 95) and repeated references to a "penny" (*ll.* 120, 294, 295), suggestions of the basis for the conquest of Mexico for its mineral wealth.

At this point in the poem, Williams calls the Mexicans "Spaniards!" (*l.* 318) before he clarifies them parenthetically as "mostly / Indians" (*ll.* 318–19). Here Williams may appear somewhat short-sighted, or even racist, about the Mexican culture; Mexicans are not simply Spaniards or Indians, a dichotomy (used in this study in its general sense of a thing or concept divided into two distinct, often contradictory, characteristics, and overtly artificial in their division) which is not lost on the critic Julio Marzán who calls the outburst a "passionate tongue-lashing ... [a] misnomer ['Spaniards!' which Williams] often used to describe Spanish-speakers in his life" (255). This clearly amplifies Williams's ambivalence (possibly too soft a word) toward his own Puerto Rican heritage, one that is fraught with class anxiety. The word choice "Spaniard" foregrounds the European roots, essentially attempting to erase all other roots.

Although the Puerto Rican culture is not interchangeable on significant levels with Mexican culture, they do contain certain general commonalities based upon historical and cultural interstices. This "misnomer" is a moment of collision between the personal (autobiography) and the stereotypical (North American social assumptions); except for sites like "his father and great Spanish writers and artists, in *The Autobiography* Williams paints Spanish-speakers mockingly, subtly invoking social preconceptions and stereotypes" (Marzán 23). Ironically, Williams is now being looked at for the complexity of his Hispanic and cultural identities by critics who occasionally fail to observe or choose to minimize some of his potentially racist assumptions.

"The Desert Music" is a conflated confrontation of Williams's complex cultural citizenship.

> Throughout the poem a catalog of antagonistic cultural symbols—Juárez and El Paso, the man-embryo, and the poet-doctor, Mexican popular music and Casals' music, empty gestures and meaningful form, the lying and the genuine, English and Spanish, "us" and "them"—haunt Williams, competing, contradicting each other, transforming him constantly while collectively composing him [Marzán 242–43].

Thus, Williams's excursion to El Paso's "sistered" city brings him face to face with oppositional options about his own identity; the bridge is truly the path to the self, possibly the self above chaos (if that is not *the* fiction).

As the poem ends, music and meaning swirl as if in a dust storm.

1. William Carlos Williams

The inclusion of scored music by Pablo Casals is a deliberate contrast to the overly sentimentalized Mexican music in the restaurant; "the continual banging of the *mariachi* music, put out for the American tourists, assailed the poet's ears" (Robinson 260). This evocation of Casals is highly suggestive of Williams's search for artistic genealogy, for

> Casals too was born of a mother from Puerto Rico, the land in which he lived and worked after the Spanish Civil War, and where he died. Being Puerto Rican and his mother's favorite musician, Casals was another Williams' alter image and a tributary, the musician always evoked by Williams' reference to the cello [Marzán 256].

There is something important in establishing mental, spiritual and cultural links between the past and the present.

Everywhere that Williams goes in Juárez, he encounters music:

>   the music! the
> *music!* as when Casals struck
> and held a deep cello tone
> and I am speechless   .
>
>   There it sat
> in the projecting angle of the bridge flange
> as I stood aghast and looked at it—
> in the half-light: shapeless or rather returned
> to its original shape, armless, legless,
> headless, packed like the pit of a fruit into
> that obscure corner — or
> a fish to swim against the stream — or
> a child in the womb prepared to imitate life,
> warding its life against
> a birth of awful promise. The music
> guards it, a mucus, a film that surrounds it,
> a benumbing ink that stains the
> sea of our minds — to hold us off — shed
> of a shape close as it can get to no shape,
> a music! a projecting music   .

> I *am* a poet! I
> am. I am. I am a poet, I reaffirmed, ashamed
>
> Now the music volleys through as in
> a lonely moment I hear it. Now it is all
> about me. The dance! The verb detaches itself
> seeking to become articulate.
>
> And I could not help thinking
> of the wonders of the brain that
> hears that music and of our
> skill sometimes to record it [*ll.* 325–54].

The figure, sighted late in the poem but evoked at the poem's beginning, ultimately brings the music — and the dance — to the foreground. Most tourists crossing this bridge, or re-crossing this bridge, might dismiss this figure, or, at the least, avoid articulating his presence; however, Williams values the "banal and trivial particulars of American life or landscape and making them universal, or revealing the universalities hidden within them" (Miller 981). In other words, Williams carries his talent for observation to Mexico. The bridge, then, between two sister cities in two separate countries is unified by the universal nature of music and dance, and the "skill sometimes to record it" (354).

The poem ends, as promised by Williams, "about a form" (*l.* 3). This returns us to the poem's beginning; the opening cry of "Wait!" (*l.* 5) indicates that the poet is at last willing to make contact with the Mexican boys begging for pennies. This moment "represents the poet's first confrontation with the aboriginal American culture that history has overlaid with civilization" (Paul 85). The brief journey to Mexico has exposed Williams to the physicality of culture and history. When the poet finally gives the children pennies, it causes "him to hear the inner music again" (Marzán 254). The act of touching, the daring to touch, initiates the journey to creativity. "Like *Paterson*, 'The Desert Music' provided a narrative thread and a journey. This time it was a journey between worlds, and the poem began literally in a no-man's land" (Mariani 126). The poem is a departure for Williams because

Mexico, not the United States, provides the poem's physical backdrop as well as the locus for him to define his role as poet. Like the form on the bridge, Williams is both shapeless and shaped by exterior forces.

"The Desert Music" is not just new; it extends the tapestry of Williams's familiar poetic landscapes. The poem's "reluctance to separate art and life, in its anti-formalism and in its refusal to intellectualize or ignore certain areas of experience" (Bertens 126) is startlingly representative of almost every aspect of Williams's *ouevre*. Consistently he uses "materials, inspiration, aesthetic, personal, and public ends" (Paul 103). Nevertheless, Paul reminds us that Williams's poem is "a demonstration of the furthest reach of [Williams's] art" (103). Such a far reach is distant from Paterson, New Jersey; indeed, the poet Charles Olson believes that "The Desert Music" is Williams's "best work … and not *Paterson*"(65) as quoted in Robert von Hallberg's *Charles Olson: The Scholar's Act*. In either case, place plays a central role in Williams's literary formation of his aesthetic identity, his personal personae.

Juárez, a place foreign to Williams, leads unexpectedly to the universal; music and dance (particularly at the site of the Other: Williams's bridge) must inevitably appropriate the poet's role as an American:

> but this, following the insensate music,
> is based on the dance:
>
>   an agony of self-realization
> bound into a whole
> by that which surrounds us.
>
>   I cannot escape
> I cannot vomit it up
>
> Only the poem!
>
> Only the made poem, the verb calls it
>   into being. [*ll*. 43–52]

The "this," presumably, is the poem, which Williams describes as "an agony of self-realization / bound into a whole" (*ll.* 45–46). Williams suggests that his self-realization, here and now, leaves him without sense. The figure exists there in front of him, indifferent to the poet's feelings but central to this poem's core of knowledge. The poem's kinesis (in its broadest sense of movement), as it opposes stasis (in its broadest sense of stagnation or non-movement), remains a rubric of potentiality. The journey to Williams's knowledge about his own suspended identity spans countries (Americans as poets and tourists reifying their own real and false truths), personal crises and poetic landscapes. Williams, as cultural geographer, recognizes boundary and boundaries. For a poet, there is always a way that being between cultures leaves one disturbed, and undisturbed — and disturbed again — because poetry makes *IT* (everything and nothing) make sense. Williams realizes that his identity (hyper–American) is a way to avoid global investment in cultural re-production. It is in Mexico that this poet allows, confronts and yields to his own conquest of creative word usages — a synecdoche for his life.

Poetry, for Williams, is the "music of survival" (*l.* 61); poetry, as basic as water, answers thirsts beyond the law, beyond borders, even beyond the physical. The desert music which inspires the dance ends about the motionless form, regressed into the shape of an egg (a fetus), "armless, legless, / headless" (*ll.* 333–34); then, suddenly, the revelatory exclamation: "I *am* a poet! I / am. I am. I am a poet" (*ll.* 345–46). The revelation, such as it is, occurs because Mexico suddenly surrounds Williams: "Mexico and the United States, grand operatic symbols of Spanish and English.... The Rio Grande (where the United States and Mexico fuse) can be the perfect symbol where this embryo can be born" (Marzán 246). The poem is born. Williams marvels at the shapeless figure, asleep between two countries, for "only to a logical mind does this reluctant primal mass seem undefined or unformed; for Williams it is 'form,' a work of art, a poet" (Marzán 257). Interestingly, Mexico proves to be a source of renewal for this most American of poets. The brief journey into Juárez (a foreign country, despite its proximity) evolves into discovery — "The Desert Music" as a complex landscape ("soulscape") of the mature, creative self. Williams's poem here, a Babel of voices and sounds, allows him to hear discordance as discourse; the silent, shapeless form reminds the poet to listen to all of the desert's music.

Mexico becomes, for Williams, an unexpected source of renewal, although it also opens up ambivalent sites of his own Hispanic identity that becomes problematized. Juárez, a place foreign to Williams, inevitably leads the poet-narrator and, by extension, his readers to universality: in music, dance and (possibly) poetry. In her essay "Dying and Living"—an apt title for one of the dominant themes of Williams's "The Desert Music"—Denise Levertov writes:

> In the poetry of William Carlos Williams, which I began to read almost as long ago as Rilke's letters and poems, there is a recurrent, indeed I sometimes feel even a dominant theme, rarely if ever spelled out but covertly present in poem after poem (and in some of his prose too)—the praise of intense, bold, essentially death-defying acts and attitudes and the sense of the paradoxical dependence of this beauty, which resides in intensity, upon the brevity of life and the inevitability of death—upon *having* a mortality to defy. Maybe this smacks of Manichean heresy, of Zoroastrian dualism—but it is not quite that; its praise is not for life as *opposed* to death but for the synthesis, life/death or death/life, the curious embrace and union of positive and negative that is the human condition—although we can perceive the condition most readily as conflict, not as synthesis [50].

This "curious embrace and union of positive and negative" is at the core of Williams's reevaluation of his life and his role as a poet as it is characterized in this poem. His personal journey into Mexico leads to a personal sense of transmutation, for Williams confronts his own sense of loss over what happens when the poetic self is not fulfilled.

For Williams, "investigating location becomes an opportunity to deconstruct the binary formations of modernity in favor of the complex, shifting social relations that produce cultures, subjects, and identities" (Kaplan 186–87). Investigating Mexico, although not *deep* Mexico, leads to an investigation into Williams's matriarchal heritage and sensibilities, which seems appropriate for this poet's psychic rebirth. One of Williams's central projects in modern American poetry has always been to lift it out of its European constricts, as well as to allow it to emerge and transcend "from a socially isolated and culturally deaf patriarchal society," to use theorist M. M. Bakhtin's words ("Epic and Novel" 11).

As stated previously, there is something important in establishing mental, spiritual and cultural links between the past and the present, as well as between the patriarchal and the matriarchal. Reclaiming and investigating the matriarchal line can be transcendant, which Williams upholds, if the individual lifts it out of the level of oppositional investigation, which Williams does. In short, Williams's ambivalence in "The Desert Music" does not originate from fear/hate/dismissal/etc. of the feminine, but, possibly, from fear/hate/dismissal/etc. of his Hispanic nature. His personal definition of Americanness is one that keeps his Hispanic American identity on the periphery; in this particular poem, Williams returns to his identity in the center of U.S. culture. The universality Williams strives for inevitably rests on a very provincial notion of universality, one that is based more upon privilege and power, such as the power of naming, than on shared human experiences which are not neatly categorized.

Williams's central project is writing home, creating what is "American" in the United States into modern poetry. Williams's journey into the foreign is a journey into his Hispanic nature, as well as his American identity — which he has so meticulously constructed. The transnational bridge that is central in the poem links two countries, indeed two sister cities, but it also links Williams's American identity with his Puerto Rican roots, with ambivalent results. The "foreign" cannot enter discourses without a profound rippling effect.

Ultimately "The Desert Music" is a work of affirmation; the sleeping, embryonic figure on the bridge comes to represent Williams, the man and the poet, and his fears — of death, of being unable to write again — as well as a potential for creative rebirth. Although he remains ambivalent about his Hispanic origins, there is a sense in the poem that something has been renewed or awakened. There is an active eye in this poem, along with an active ear. "Multiplicity, the listing of things without violating their particular existence, becomes a deliberate strategy" (Collecott 120). In order to avoid "violating" the world in which the poet finds himself, Williams allows many voices to be heard in this work. Even as a piece of music may incorporate the many sounds of different instruments, Williams's long poem is inclusive of the exterior and interior sounds he encounters in Mexico.

Theorist Homi K. Bhabha writes that "cultural difference emerges from the borderline moment of translation" (314). Translation is the art of transferring words in one language into another, an inexact process at best. This bilingualness becomes even more problematic for Williams as his matriarchal affiliation with Spanish and his patriarchal investment in the English language suddenly coexist in material ways in this Juárez-inspired poem. He is physically and intellectually on the "borderline" and suddenly aware of cultural difference. This poem about Mexico brings Williams back to life; the journey to Mexico forces him to confront outsidedness (the Other) within his own complex identity, something rich he carries back with him.

It is important to remember that this confrontation takes place within a poem, that Williams works within this literary genre to capture the music of everyday experience even as it becomes negotiated by his own privilege as a poet. This act of composition is ultimately a compound project, one that offers the temptation of the monologue.

In "The Desert Music," the technique of multi-voicing and Williams's own sites of bewilderment and affiliation both provide a means by which to locate himself within discourses of "the masses." The masses here, perhaps ironically, are participants and heirs of the old world of Williams's Spanish-influenced childhood; remember, the poet's first book of poems was entitled *Al Que Quiere* ("to whoever wants to" or "to whoever desires to"). This book title's casualness disguises Williams's investment in personal experiences as the sites of perception when they become sources of meditation. These sources contain the potential for real transformative powers. "*Duende* ... was what Williams also interpreted as the creative spirit or fecund earth-force by which Washington or Thomas Merton becomes truly American; *duende* was the Andalusian word for that Dionysian presence, the fire in the heart, that Williams identified as Carlos" (Marzán 190). This "fire in the heart" energizes the aging and ill poet; with what time is left to him, Williams wants to continue at his work while retaining his sense of humor.

> So this is William
> Carlos Williams, the poet.
>
> Floss and I had half consumed
> our quartered hearts of lettuce before
> we noticed the others hadn't touched theirs
> You seem quite normal. Can you tell me? Why
> does one want to write a poem?
>
> Because it's there to be written.
>
> Oh. A matter of inspiration then?
>
> Of necessity [*ll.* 272–81]

Necessity, of course, is a concept linked inextricably to an individual's priorities and notions of values. For Williams, this excursion into Mexico is quite the unexpected adventure; he encounters his past and present without warning. Bakhtin writes that "one can relate to the past in a familiar way.... But in so doing we ignore the presentness of the present and the pastness of the past" ("Epic and Novel" 14). Williams in "The Desert Music" becomes aware that he is the bridge between his past and the general American present, a position that is as much about the powers of the poet as it is about a specific individual's life experiences. Williams, in this poem, cannot ignore the long journey toward the "Carlos" that is his middle name; his investigative systems must accommodate his own compounded identity.

Just as music becomes linked to dance in this poem, Williams's contact with the Mexican culture reaffirms the important place poetry holds in his life, for it is touch and smell and keen observation. Marzán suggests that "a writer's experience is always foreign, isolated and unique, always needing to be translated into the local currency" (264). In being in Mexico, but not of Mexico, Williams has the privilege of distance, and yet his own ethnicity problematizes this distancing. Only when he becomes a poet and writes home does Williams become his own translator; links with those about him (and by implication his readers) become foregrounded.

>   I *am* a poet! I
> am. I am. I am a poet, I reaffirmed, ashamed
> [... ... ...]
>   And I could not help thinking
>   of the wonders of the brain that
>   hears that music and of our
>   skill sometimes to record it [*ll.* 345–54].

Whether the shame articulated here confronts his ambivalence about Hispanic culture or his own failure to realize that he is still alive and creative is unclear; perhaps, on some level, it addresses both. The "skill sometimes to record it" (*l.* 354), however, is still very active for Williams, and Mexico is the proving ground for this provocative realization.

2

Jack Kerouac

Jack Kerouac visited Mexico several times, and some of those visits were rather extended which allowed him greater experiential and psychic interaction. Even on brief trips, Kerouac's intensity in regard to his artistic production characterizes those trips as significant events for his prose writing and on, at least, one occasion his poetry writing. "During August and the first half of September 1955, he composed 242 choruses" (Nicosia 480), which comprise his blues-chorus sequence entitled *Mexico City Blues*.* One of the overall, significant elements that characterizes this book of poems is that there is less of a textual presence of Mexico than a reader might assume, given the volume's title. Indeed, Mexico, even when textually present, is often absent in terms of Kerouac representing and commenting upon the country's contemporary political and cultural realities; Mexico's pre-colonial history is frequently alluded to, if only in one word or name, but twentieth-century Mexico, the actual Mexico that Kerouac would have found all around him during the writing of *Mexico City Blues*, is harder to find here.

Hard to find, yes, but the Mexico exterior to the Mexico City of

---

**Poems about Mexico can be found in* Heaven and Other Poems *and* Pomes All Sizes, *as well as his unpublished poetry manuscripts. Until a comprehensive collection of Kerouac's poetry is done, including dates of composition, I must limit myself, in this study, to the works that comprise* Mexico City Blues. *It is encouraging, I must state, that other works exist, or may come to light, which will one day permit me to expand upon these initial observations and, potentially, challenge my overall assumptions.*

the 1950s does appear in Kerouac's poems in this volume. It appears in ways that allow readings of the concept of the foreign as both separate and linked to Kerouac's own complex role as American citizen. "The tourist is a kind of contemporary pilgrim, seeking authenticity in other 'times' and other 'places' away from that person's everyday life" (Urry 9). Kerouac certainly was on a pilgrimage to another place, but also a spiritual pilgrimage. *Mexico City Blues*, then, is not invested in location so much as in meditation, geography often yielding to metaphysics throughout numerous choruses. This collection of poetry is "an influential volume among poets of Kerouac's era, taking Eastern spirituality and giving it presence in American poetics, as well as in the American ecological movement" (Swartz 21); *Mexico City Blues* is a challenging text, to say the least, for it is extremely fluid and highly impressionistic in terms of its author's own methods of mythopoetic composition and an individualized interpretation of Buddhism.

Kerouac's foray into Mexico, which inspires *Mexico City Blues*, covers a wide range of "gringo" experiences* that often include acceptance of difference; fetishization of a foreign culture and its misread semiotics; ironically, fear of difference; and dismissal of social realities and historical complexities. It is important to keep in mind that Kerouac was no typical tourist, because he arrives in Mexico as an emerging writer seeking to establish his own voice and subject material. Kerouac's work, ideally, sought escape from the dichotomy of tourists versus locals. His journey into Mexico, surely, was intended to provide an intense experience through which to reconsider place in his own country and texts; Kerouac "always questioned his place in the world" (Wilson 89). Kerouac, like the other Beats, specifically questioned their places in 1950s America. Michael Elliott in *The Day Before Yesterday* characterizes the situation as "a sort of underground opposition in (and to) the dispensation of the 1950s. That opposition included artists and

---

By "gringo" experience(s) I mean a complex set of reactions to the "foreign" which include: simplifying everyday realities, conflating diversity's complexities, displaying a lack of interest in the Spanish language, primitivizing the lives of the Mexicans, sensationalizing the different and keeping a distance from ordinary people and overemphasizing the spectacle(s). "Gringo" is a useful term to name the typical tourist, the casual observer, in which the baggage of ethnocentrism significantly weighs down the writer.

Beats, Old Left unionists and communists, poets and academics" (144). Mexico, it seems, might allow Kerouac the physical distance from which to re-look at and re-think through his relationship(s) with his own country and his own texts.

Unlike many of his contemporaries who "consciously indulged oppositional ideas" (Lhamon 5), Kerouac assumably goes to Mexico to investigate the possible rewards to be gained through opening up his work to greater textual plurality and to specifically explore his trope of the outsider. Steve Wilson reminds us, "Kerouac's interest in the 'outsider' is itself an intriguing and complicated tangle of emotions for him as he sets out on his quest for authenticity" (79). Kerouac, it seems, was less invested in the authenticity of Mexico than in using that country as a means of writing America, perhaps finding his own self authenticity. Here I disagree with Barry Gifford and Lawrence Lee who state in *Jack's Book: An Oral Biography of Jack Kerouac* that "Ginsberg and Burroughs had gone to the trouble of leaving the country in obligatory literary fashion, looking back on America with the perspective offered by Mexico, Panama, or North Africa. When Jack traveled, his mind's eye was busy recording the at-hand. He did not look over his shoulder" (231). I would have to go so far as to say that in *Mexico City Blues*, Kerouac rarely *stops* looking "over his shoulder." The overall absence of Mexico, and its realities, is a reflection of Kerouac's unconscious investment in writing *to* home, to a United States with which the Beats were positioned as disrupters of dominant or mainstream culture since the late 1940s. The Beats' "aversion to the dominant symbols of postwar American might was not an outright rejection of the 'American Way of Life,' but a reconfiguration of the terms" (Lardas 178).

Being away from the United States, Kerouac hoped to explore polyvocality, multi-voicing, but almost inevitably he fell back into a dichotomous discourse, returning to that requisite writing strategy deployed by the Beats as a response to their imposed or self-imposed space outside of mainstream society. The Beat movement is generally recognized as anti–Establishment; naturally, the discourse of opposition implies engagement with that which one is against. Kerouac, for one, could not break out of this interconnection.

When the United States began to come to terms with the diverse nature of its greater society, an insular American hegemony began to crumble and give way to the upheaval of the 1960s. It was a period of national and individual psychic crises, ones without easy or immediate resolutions. Kerouac escaped into alcoholism for many profound reasons, including the fact that he was a perpetual outsider in U.S. culture, partly due to his French-Canadian heritage. In *Mexico City Blues*, interestingly, we see glimpses of Kerouac interrogating his own multicultural American identity and possibly beginning to come to terms with it: "English was his second language; as a boy he had spoken joual, the dialect of the French Canadians" (Halberstam 299). Kerouac's restlessness then can be traced not only to social and political conditions, but to his own outsider status located within his genealogy. In a September 8, 1950 letter to Yvonne Le Maitre, who reviewed *The Town and the City*, Kerouac writes "Your mention of my mother and father warmed my heart. Because I cannot write my native language and have no native home any more, and am amazed by that horrible homelessness all French-Canadians abroad in America have" (*Selected Letters* 228). This sense of homelessness eventually leads Kerouac to a Mexico that could lead him to a desired and desirable universal place of mind. In other words, by attempting to find his own "primitive" paradise, "his Mecca promises finally to be Mexico City" (Foster 43), this Beat "king" begins to confront the outsider within himself and inevitably begins to confront the Other, the outsider, in Mexico.

Kerouac's own ambivalence toward his French-Canadian identity may have led to his attempts to overcompensate for the racism of the dominant culture (a primary Beat project) and his failure in achieving those ideals on a day-to-day basis. "The Beats, as they came to be known, revered those who were different, those who lived outside the system.... They believed that blacks were somehow freer, less burdened by the restraints of straight America" (Halberstam 300). To be outside of the system, as many African American and other American minorities were then (and many still are now), is significantly more voluntary in Kerouac's case, which ultimately restricts and conflates complex identity issues into static notions of race and ethnicity. Kerouac's Beat status and identification with groups considered outsiders repeats the autobiographical alienation informed by his French-Canadian heritage. Nancy McCampbell Grace reminds us that it is "critical that we not lose sight of Kerouac's hybrid status.... [Kerouac's] history that bequethed him a complicated identity, one which transformed his own Causasian heritage into something of a sinister monolith, a force to be feared and shunned but nonetheless revered" (94). Thus, Kerouac was a stranger in U.S. society on many levels, but not all of those levels may have been fully articulated or claimed.

Language has always played an important role in Kerouac's life. "He was raised speaking the local French-Canadian dialect, joual, the largely working class and oral tradition he continued to use with his mother throughout his life" (Douglas 30). It has been shown that "there were five French parishes alone in Lowell, a French language newspaper and schools where all the lessons were in French" (S. Turner 29). This bilingual experience locates an early site of struggle where Kerouac, the child, attempts to belong to a culture and its necessary citizenship. Steve Turner in his book *Angelheaded Hipster: A Life of Jack Kerouac* emphasizes that

> Up until the age of five Jack spoke nothing but French, and even during his teenage years he had trouble understanding English if it was spoken too fast. He was aware at an early age of being a foreigner in his own country, and the theme of alienation, of searching for his true home, would pervade his writing [31].

What hasn't been noticed in much of the criticism about Kerouac is that the searching for "his true home" parallels his explorations into language. "Linguistically, Kerouac always led a double life; the idiom of his novels was American English but his imagination was joual" (Douglas 30–31). In a letter written to Neal Cassady, dated December 28, 1950, Kerouac's "second birth" replicates the conditions of his earlier incarnation as a French Canadian on U.S. soil: "I see the sun. And now, and soon, you will know why I saw 'the house I was born in' in Mexico, won't you?—and it will all be clear as day. And Mexico because of the sun, the drowse, the ah-bwa-ah-bwa of their own tongue" (*Selected Letters* 255). The sound of the language is the meaning, an insight which provides access then to the title *Mexico City Blues* and its attendant investment in jazz and blues structures, his "spontaneous method" (Theado 71) practiced in all his works, but practiced "with words, as [Kerouac] says in his introduction to *Mexico City Blues*" (Theado 71). Here we could substitute the "ah-bwa-ah-bwa of their own tongue" (*Selected Letters* 255) to Kerouac's own tongues, both joual and English; now in this poetry collection, adding Spanish to the mix foregrounds the polyvocality available in locations defined by geography and poetry. His search for a true home, if only through language, parallels his explorations into notions of Mexican identity, however superficially.

This anxiety over identity sometimes translates as that most insular of hegemonic American activities, racism. Kerouac's simplification and trivialization of the Other, usually denoted by racial status, links him to the greater American project of policing arbitrary dichotomies, such as divisions between black and white Americans.

> Kerouac tried to enhance and ennoble his position as a *voluntary* social outsider by linking himself to the historical status of African Americans as *forced* outsiders and victims of white oppression. Discursively, Kerouac made this connection by raiding African American culture for its method of expressing the experience of this oppression and its strategy for surviving it [Panish 121].

Mexico City Blues cannot be dismissed or reduced to an act of "raiding," for the poetry collection is not simply a map of romantic choices but rather a messy acknowledgment of simultaneous discourses at work. The African-American question in Kerouac's works insists on a historical re-reading that must consider the gravity of this writer's choice to volunteer to hold an outsider's position, a linking to the foreigner as a simplified textuality of race, power and cultural production.

Certainly the Mexico poems foreground an inclusivity that may be categorized as less "racist" than his prose, writing which allows and indeed features systems of oppression while the poems map interior spaces. Although Wilson points out that it is common for critics to point fingers at Kerouac's racism (77), racism in U.S. society permeated the 1950s (but obviously not only that decade); Kerouac, like many of the Beats, fetishized the Other within U.S. society and in Mexico: African

Americans, Mexican Americans and Mexicans, among others. Ironically, Kerouac is admitting the social, political and cultural presence and vitality of these groups even as he uses mainstream categories and stereotypes that return these groups to the status of marginalization.

> Even on the dawn (and later, in the midst) of the Civil Rights Movement, white authors, such as Jack Kerouac, who positioned themselves on the outside of the social and literary mainstream — that is, contiguous with, if not intersecting those groups who had been forced outside — were not any closer than writers to previous generations ... to representing America's oppressed minorities in ways that respected those groups and traditions. Not recognizing their own complicity in perpetuating racist ideology, Kerouac and others continued the tradition of primitivizing and romanticizing the experiences of racial minorities (particularly African Americans) and raiding their culture and contemporary experience for the purpose of enhancing their own position as white outsiders [Panish 107–08].

I wonder if Kerouac, and perhaps the other Beat writers, were aware of the danger of "enhancing" their positions as outsiders at the costs of marginalized groups. In Kerouac's essay "Mexico Fellaheen," he writes: "you can find it [in Mexico], this feeling, this fellaheen feeling about life, that timeless gayety of people not involved in great cultural and civilization issues" (22). Note how Kerouac, an outsider in Mexico, switches positions with the citizens of that country and adopts or assumes the power of interpretation over Mexico's culture and civilization.

Here, Kerouac is not seeing Mexicans as a means to enhance his career as a spokesperson for the margins, but rather fails to see Mexicans in the context of their own contemporary, protean realities. Here racism is revealed to be a complex phenomenon. I want to be clear that although racist notions may inform some of the choruses in *Mexico City Blues*, whether they are explicit or not, these notions do not authorize a simple dismissal of Kerouac's poems for there is still much to be found in the work here, including the extent of the "liberalism" associated with the Beats (excluding Kerouac's later years). "Not always as 'liberal' as we might wish today, the Beats nevertheless voluntarily cast themselves into the vortex of cultural diversity long before it became socially acceptable" (Wilson 90). In investigating the nature of Mexico and how it may be viewed from U.S. perspectives, racism, exoticism ("local color"), fetishization and primitivism are important keys to getting at American identity formations. This makes Kerouac's work pivotal to my project because in *Mexico City Blues*, to use Bakhtin's concept, "a verbal-ideological center is to be found at the center of organization where all levels intersect. The different levels are to varying degrees distant from this authorial center" ("From the Prehistory" 48–49). The "ah-bwa-ah-bwa" of the Mexican language (Kerouac, *Selected Letters* 255), then, is not mere native gibberish but an impacted system of vocality which here, in *Mexico City Blues*, reveals as much about the listeners as the speakers. Kerouac opens up the spaces of his English-language words to other vocalities, and here Bakhtin reminds us that "one's own language is never a single language" ("From the Prehistory" 66), but Kerouac attempts to retain his own position at the center of the language-scape he finds in Mexico.

In the early years of the 1950s, Kerouac, like other Beat artists, generally sought a utopian model upon which to base their criticisms of the United States; "the Beats viewed their contemporary America as disconnected from its natural source" (Lardas 133). *Mexico City Blues*, as the book's title suggests, is located in the foreign, the urban and is informed by the music from the margin. What Foster says about Kerouac's *On the Road* is applicable to this poetry collection; he states that Kerouac, the author, positions himself in the role of "a guide to ways out of a conformist civilization — but in the end [*On the Road*] admits that all these roads lead back to where they began" (43), which could just as easily apply to *Mexico City Blues*. As much as Michael McClure in the documentary *What Happened to Jack Kerouac?* insists that "*Mexico City Blues* is the great religious poem so far in the twentieth century," Kerouac does not seek another world or faraway heaven, but rather in these choruses the roads are infused with a sense of return to the United States. Throughout Kerouac's writing career, he deployed a strategy that was "not stream of consciousness, something written to suggest the mental processes of a character, but what might be termed stream of attention since the passage records a process which is conscious, directed, and focused on the physical world" (Hunt 173).

This "stream of attention" should constantly reveal the world of the daily, but in this collection the daily world of Mexico is not usually revealed, much less the precapitalist utopia that Kerouac so wanted Mexico to be.

> Jack's Mexico City is the heart of fellaheen country [in *Tristessa*], a land cut off from the social hierarchy dominating the United States. In *On the Road*, he calls Mexico the place where we "will finally learn ourselves" (1979, 280), and in *Tristessa*, one of those lessons seems to be that since America has failed its own people a classless society is possible only where the illusions of black and white blend and are negated by brown [McCampbell Grace 113].

What is revealed, then, is his proclivity to write poems to America (the United States), a potential site of an unlovable paradise. When Gerald Nicosia makes the following statement he does not fully articulate the implications of his interesting observation: "*Mexico City Blues* is a Buddhist book that finally talks itself back to a Christian love of life" (480). *Mexico City Blues* as a whole has certainly captured the critics' "stream of attention." In addition to McClure and Nicosia, the poetry collection has been wildly categorized and pigeon-holed; it has been labeled "playful and light" (Foster 64); "[radiating] an all-inclusiveness" (Weinreich 64); "universally damned by his reviewers because of its sloppiness and vacuity" and a work of "echolalic verbiage" (Hipkiss 80–81); "difficult to read" (Powell 1); "an echoic, locomotive poetic" and a "riddling infusion of high-speed, steam powered romance" (Powell 3–4); and, Gary Snyder's understated characterization holds that they "are interesting contemporary Buddhist poems" (Gifford 211). Ultimately, Nicosia's notion is central: *Mexico City Blues* is "a Buddhist book that finally talks itself back to a Christian love of life" (480).

Kerouac returns to his notion of Christian love because Kerouac always seems *to return*: to his original religion (Catholicism), to his home town (Lowell, Massachusetts) and to his mother (perhaps to avoid his allegedly confused sexual orientation). "Kerouac was always able to (and often did) return from his wild escapades to his doting mother" (Wilson 89). Kerouac's return to Christianity is, also, an escape from "utopia," a Mexico where "marijuana is stronger, the women easier to come by, and the people live for the pleasures of the day. They even find the smell of dirt and bugs pleasanter in Mexico" (Hipkiss 6), as theatricalized in *On the Road*. His status as an outsider becomes co-opted by capitalism, and not spirituality, as he becomes famous and begins to have access to the trappings of media and literary attentions. His experiences of being located in the First World are profoundly reinforced by his various stays in the Third World, particularly Mexico. Kerouac's travels and his reporting of his experiences in Mexico are primarily reinforcing the dialectical relationship with the American mainstream that characterizes his writing career. Mexico impresses him not because it is Mexico, but because it is *not* the United States. It is the non–First World, which could be Central America, Africa or almost anywhere.

As Kerouac experiences Mexico, "home" and "self," as issues, become foregrounded in his poems. In the process of being in Mexico, he appears to redefine his own citizenship. Throughout *Mexico City Blues* we see occasional glimpses of Kerouac's awareness of connections between being French Canadian and being a Mexican Indian. The following anecdote illustrates both Kerouac's hunger for connection and apparent naïveté of history:

> Jack kept scribbling in his notebook throughout the evening, much to the amusement of the Indians. Unlike Casteñada, he wasn't trying to understand the Indians. He wasn't even trying very hard to get them to understand him. He shoved his notebook at the Indians forcing them to read his descriptions of the hut where Enrique had taken him and his sensations lighting up the marijuana and opium cigarettes. He insisted they could understand each other's language because Jack was an Indian too. His great-great-grandmother had been a Canadian Indian [Charters 158].

Once again, language plays an important role: the possibility and necessity of transmitted knowledge. Note also the presence of his "notebook," which is not a diary and yet very personal. In forcing the Indians to read a selected entry, Kerouac is offering not only his words but the experiences located in his words. Whether or not the Indians found any use for this writing is not as significant as the observation that once again Kerouac was rewriting the world through his own stream of attention.

To write the everyday realities of Mexico might demand seeing beyond the superficial gaze, and that process, inevitably, requires a number of emotive, subjective skills foregrounded in the writer's arsenal, such as the art of noting details, valuing associative powers of the specific, and allowing new formations of priorities. *Mexico City Blues* is framed by Mexico — indeed Mexico City — but it is a site as much about perception and meditation as it is a geographical and cultural intersection. "When [Kerouac] arrived in Mexico City in the summer of 1955, he wrote his long poem *Mexico City Blues,* his first artistic attempt to convey his Buddhist-inspired visions," according to Mark Theado in *Understanding Jack Kerouac*. What remains at the center of *Mexico City Blues*, inevitably, is Kerouac's own American identity; the book generally appears to be a book of American blues poems almost incidentally written in Mexico City.

Mexico as an actual country, a specific place, is first mentioned in the "9th Chorus," but in this chorus it is not mentioned clearly, "directly." I qualify directly because it does not appear equivalent to the several places mentioned in the poem — Death Valley, Washington DC, New Orleans, Australia and Portugal — but as a sort of state or condition where "heroines" dwell: "— The Heroines of Cathedral / Fellaheen Mexico —" (*ll.* 12–13). Here Mexico becomes attached to Kerouac's mystical (and mythical) conception of the "fellaheen," which S. Turner explains as "a special reverence to the poor and discarded — the 'desolation angels' and 'fellaheed'— because [Kerouac] believed that they were open to revelations that others weren't" (69). These prophets, inevitably, have the power to define the experiential in terms of location, at least through Kerouac's lens.

Location seems central in the "9th Chorus," where Mexico becomes almost personified, as part of an appositive to "The Giant Angels / In the Washington D C Blue Sky" (*ll.* 10–11), but what are we, as readers of this text, to make of the mere naming of a place? Naming places, or historical monuments or individuals, in Mexican history, is analogous to the concept of looking without seeing; this poetry collection does not locate Kerouac in Mexico so much as lend him a place from which to depart. This naming of an actual Mexico is done sparsely in Kerouac's *Mexico City Blues*; furthermore, it often emerges without significant context and disappears just as swiftly and seems rarely missed.

Naming, through Whitmanesque cataloging, can help to depict the depth and breadth of a culture. The potential to capture such reality, or realities, of Mexico permeates *Mexico City Blues*, but it never seems to come to fruition, partly because Kerouac cannot escape the simplified dialectics which he has packed for this trip. In his letter of June 3, 1952, to Carolyn Cassady, Kerouac writes: "Eternity is the only thing on my mind permanently, and you are a part of it. One good thing about Mexico, you just get high and dig eternity every day." (*Selected Letters* 364). Note how getting high also means an abandonment of the actual.

Kerouac's self-involvement is at odds with the potential adventures and lessons all about him in a foreign country. The only streets that seem to be presented in *Mexico City Blues* are the ones in his imagination which seem to be generic streets, possibly generic U.S. streets. This abstraction contributes to the overall absence of Mexico in these bluesy, Buddhist-inspired rifts. Significantly, not only is Mexico rarely present, but there is virtually nothing specific to Mexico City here, which gives pause about the collection's overall title. Ultimately, then, "Jack's faith in passion and primitivism" (S. Turner 178) is less about location, as in Mexico City, than about arriving there or departing from there by any road available (even if only the road maps are in his mind).

In the following choruses, Kerouac does a bit more than just use the word "Mexico" or "Mexican"; instead, he refers to Aztecs and other historical signifiers, although not always with the understanding that the past is intricately linked to the present. There is no sense of a Bakhtinian "new zone ... the zone of maximal contact with the present (with contemporary reality) in all its openendedness" (Bakhtin, "Epic and Novel" 11). Similarly, the "13th Chorus" and the "14th Chorus" fall into this pattern of "close-endedness."

In the "13th Chorus," there is a mention of "Popocatapetl's / Hungry mouth" (*ll.* 22–23). The mention of this holy Aztec mountain does go beyond mere evocation, but mostly because of the final line that connotes the bloody history of the Aztec empire. The poem begins with that same connotation of bloody history, but on a more comical note: "I caught a cold / From the sun / When they tore my heart out / At the top of the pyramid" (*ll*. 1–4). Human sacrifice is less of a cultural phenomenon than a literary one here, the phrase "my heart" privileging the individual over ritual. Seemingly, the Aztecs are mentioned more directly in line 20 of the same chorus, where their presence — as "old Sour Azteca" — is characterized as hovering over "Saloons" (*l.* 19). Kerouac seems to sense a haunting in this land, but associates it with the social aspects of drinking by contemporary tourists and locals. Another curiosity in the "13th Chorus" occurs earlier in the chorus, in line seven, which presents the reader with the first two syllables of the "Fellaheen," as well as the monosyllables "Ack Ack" that may be allusions to the vocalized "Azteca" or may be part of another train of thought. Jones states that ultimately, the repetitions of "ack" in the collection serve as rhymes to the nickname "Jack," which in turn rhymes with "Kerouac" (93). Jones offers up this chorus, as well as the 119th and the 137th as evidence for that, but in the 119th the monosyllable appears only as the ultimate syllable in "Kallaquack," which is not his nickname, but does admittedly seem a play on his name.

In the "137th Chorus," the monosyllable "ack" as an intact unit dissolves, and here Kerouac offers us the first two lines of the chorus as: "AZTEC BLUES / 'A kek Horrac'" (*ll*. 1–2), which may be a sense of play he is taking with his name but also connects with the pronunciation of "Aztec." Note again how sound is the meaning instead of the narrative. Also, "Aztec" and "blues" are aligned as somehow linkages, words that refer to the title of the collection. It is as if the historical figures of the Aztecs and the historical bases of the African-American music that form the blues begin to collide in the mind of this very American writer who seems to be quoting a ghost or a disembodied voice, "'A kek Horrac'" (*ll*. 1–2).

Immediately following the "13th Chorus" is the mention in the "14th Chorus" of "Teotihuacan"; this Aztec god of sacrifice appears almost midway through the poem, and once again it clearly adds to the connotation of ancient rituals involving human sacrifice. Indeed in line 10, there is a direct reference to such a thing; Kerouac states: "They'll eat your heart alive." In fact the allusions to the blood sacrifices of humans strongly connect the "13th Chorus" to the "14th Chorus." This ritualized act of communal cruelty strangely contradicts many of Kerouac's romantic ideas of Mexico as utopia. Kerouac's "childlike faith is a realm of innocent goodness from which we come and to which we return" (Hipkiss 6). The idea of blood is not the same as actual or historical blood; in fact, in his essay "Mexico Fellaheen," Kerouac has a very visceral and philosophical reaction to a bullfight which he witnesses; he writes: "And I saw how everybody dies and nobody's going to care, I felt how awful it is to live just so you can die like a bull trapped in a screaming human ring" (33). Here Kerouac identifies with the bull or the victim in ways that he does not identify with any of the suffering masses in the streets of Mexico. Is Kerouac, the artist, ever truly naked to himself in the dream streets of his mythologized Mexico and, specifically, Mexico City?

In one of the last essays Kerouac wrote and published, interestingly titled "The First Word," he writes about writing: "If you don't stick to what you first thought, and to the words the thought brought, what's the sense of bothering with it anyway…?" (46–47). This advice seems helpful to readers of the choruses in *Mexico City Blues,* which resists a close reading, partly because it lacks almost any dominant narrative and partly because it may ultimately have no structural center. To call each poem a chorus or to refer to them as jazz or blues constructions is to privilege improvisation as both subject and form. "Kerouac's improvisations, repetitions, stuttering starts and stops, insistence on coexisting with the world as it is, and love of late-night performance all came directly from the jazz worlds he entered on both coasts and both banks of the Mississippi River" (Lhamon 70). It is helpful for the reader to approach the choruses as a series of words that thoughts bring. The choruses remain that elusive and that impressionistic, which are both their literary strengths and their difficulties.

In the first several choruses, there are only hints of Mexico or "Mexicanness," and these take the mere form of two Spanish words in two separate poems among the first eight poems. The word for "eye" in Spanish, *ojo,* appears in its exclamatory form in the penultimate line of the poem as a colloquialism for "watch out" or "Look!" Jones calls attention to the sprinkling of Spanish words throughout the poems, and categorizes their primary uses as "the sound effects the Spanish language provides, the opportunity life in an ancient society gives the singer to illustrate his views on reincarnation, and the images foreign landscape and folkways contribute to the surrealism of the poem" (62). Jones also admits they are a superficial binding agent to Mexico (61), which surely they are on one level.

Kerouac's use of individual Spanish words, appearing quite infrequently in certain sections of *Mexico City Blues*, certainly reinforce "local" color; also, they do associatively connect the Spanish language to the English language, just as Kerouac is trying to bridge these two cultures within himself. Jones is right to classify them as sound effects, for that is one of the primary elements of language in all the choruses, with its English words as well as its Spanish words. It is particularly important to remember that Kerouac had a significant lack of knowledge of the Spanish language. In this chorus and many of the others, the interjection of Spanish words or phrases — even if misspelled or bastardized — are intended as moments of multi-voicing, the recognition of other voices in the air besides his own voice. Comprehension is as much about hearing the music in individual words or phrases as in how these words operate within their own specific linguistic systems. The use of Spanish words or phrases clearly operate within a "different tongue" or "different speech" that interrupts the univocal thoughts of the poems' narrator whose dominant language is English (albeit informed by his French-Canadian childhood).

In the "3rd Chorus," the interjection of "Ojo!" (*l.* 22) functions as central to the poem's warning about the climbing U.S. debt, which this poem states is at "$275,000,000,000.00.... Two hundred and seventy five billion / dollars in debt" (*ll.* 11–14). Both Kerouac and Mexico, however subtly in the background, are admonishing the United States to attend to its various debts, which are certainly not only monetary. The occasional use of Spanish words in some of the choruses are potential moments of multi-voicing. These moments break through Kerouac's univocal Beat stance and open up a new space, which can be viewed as an extension of the overall, revolutionary Beat impulse to "[urge] changes in society" (Berry 93). Language itself had to be opened up, even as the United States began to solidify its global interactions in the wake of World War II. In fiction *and* poetry "there was emerging by the early fifties a deep dissatisfaction with the hermetic spaces modernism had constructed for itself " (Lhamon 100). Often, Kerouac's multi-voicing is subtle, as in the "5th Chorus," whose last two lines read: "If you know what I / p a l a b r a" (*ll.* 22–23). Here multi-voicing opens up the narrator's language to layers of signification. Kerouac is searching for just the right word, typographically spatialized as "p a l a b r a," or perhaps he is using the Spanish word for "word" as something closer to the verb infinitive "to mean," as in "If you know what I mean?" In any case, interrupting or complicating his English thoughts with a Spanish word adds at least another layer of meaning, particularly as the Spanish word concludes this chorus. Kerouac is returned to Mexico after his interior journeys, a return to a welcomed foreignness. His thoughts here, as this chorus wraps up, become significantly less univocal: a recognition that English is not the only language by which the world may be interpreted.

It is not until the "9th Chorus" that Mexico is alluded to, even if it is not mentioned directly. Jones qualifies this section as one about "Cathedral Indians" commenting on the great cities of the world (63); "the pidgin Spanish," he states, "signifies a melding of cultures" (63). Jones, then, might agree that Kerouac's occasional use of Spanish words can be characterized as brief, subtle moments of multi-voicing which advance this Beat poet's project of breaking through his own univocal language, his vantage point as an "American." What Jones does not go on to consider are the cultural and political implications of simplifying language into "pidgin," a term which suggests a bastardization of dominant discourse without finding value in communication within this group. To reduce Spanish words to "pidgin," for Kerouac, is not only to return language to sound but to return to notions of the primitive, and to the ahistorical nature of language systems: "The primitive does what we ask it to do. Voiceless, it lets us speak for it. It is our ventriloquist's dummy — or so we like to think" (Torgovnick 9). Ironically, then, the "civilized" person is ever listening for his or her own language in the mouths of outsiders.

The "12th Chorus" is the first important poem about Mexico in *Mexico City Blues*, which I characterize as a "major Mexican chorus" because here Mexico appears to be something more than an abstract concept; furthermore, it is important because Kerouac makes one of his strongest links between the "foreign" culture of Mexico and his own French-Canadian identity. This link between the outsider within him and the Mexican Indians becomes conflated in the narrator's mind and forms the basis of the "12th Chorus." Kerouac hears the "Indian songs in Mexico" (*l.* 1), which remind him of "the little French Canuckian / songs my mother sings—" (*ll.* 5–6). To him they sound like "Indian Roundelays—" (*l.* 7), songs that once again link two conflicting interpretive systems: the native and the European as expressed through a formalized poetry, the opposite of Indian songs and Kerouac's blues.

From this point forward, until almost the end of the chorus, Kerouac as narrator hears a string of nonsense words, as if part of a children's nursery rhyme, until finally this adolescent rondelet ends, almost predictably, with revelations about mothers: "(ONLY THE MOTHERS ARE HAPPY)" (*l.* 17). This statement clearly comes outside of the catalog of nonsense words; its capital letters and parenthetical structure reinforce that idea. Also, the penultimate line makes a move away from the nonsense to give the narrator some distance; in that line, Kerouac seems to qualify what has just preceded it as "Aztec squeaks" (*l.* 16). That last line, as a statement, seems plain enough superficially; juxtaposed against the children singing and his own memories of children's songs, Kerouac seems to be implying that he was not happy as a child. Perhaps he takes that so far as to characterize all children as unhappy, which adds a darker (historical) tone to the phrase "Aztec squeaks." This chorus reinforces the following observation: "Primitives are like children, the tropes say. Primitives are our untamed selves, our id forces—libidinous, irrational, violent, dangerous" (Torgovnick 8). This notion of the "untamed" self positions this poetry collection as a conscious attempt to look at the subconscious, the site of childhood, puberty and possibly, also, an adulthood full of myths and mainstream morality.

In the "12th Chorus," the squeaks themselves seem to be the

Indian children's songs, but they also may characterize Kerouac's own childhood, the French-Canadian songs of his own past. Thus, here, the cultures are conflated, first made equal to each other and then blurred together. The primitive, in its idealized isolation, is at the opposite end of the spectrum from Kerouac's troubled and over-civilized New England. It is useful to remember this writer's beginnings: "Let us begin by imagining an extremely intelligent and morbidly sensitive man born into an ethnic minority group with its own language in a decaying city in a decaying region that had earlier been the industrial and cultural center of the country" (French 116–17). Here it seems apparent that Kerouac has an articulated recognition of his own complicated identity as a French Canadian in U.S. society, and consequently this recognition places him temporarily outside of the dominant English-speaking culture.

Kerouac's "12th Chorus" falls within the realm of trying to make a connection; although the narrator relates some local color, he is clearly trying to connect to the foreign culture around him. One surprising result of this writing strategy is that Kerouac loses a bit of his self-consciousness as a writer and makes an important connection to his own childhood. The hegemony of U.S. culture with which Kerouac was often in battle disappears here. Instead, the chorus opens up to polyvocality, which initiates a renegotiation with his own cultural identity. Here, the Mexican-Indian children are just like him; they are too busy singing to be concerned whether someone has exoticized them or not. Although the children appear to be present in the poem, they do not acknowledge the poet-narrator; he remains at the center of his own discourse. Kerouac literalizes the notion of "the unfolding moment" by becoming aware of himself on many levels. His "writing is an attempt to discover form, not to imitate it, and to discover experience in the act of writing about it" (Weinreich 4). Writing, meditation and experience are often indistinguishable from each other in this chorus.

The psychic bridge that Kerouac crosses in this chorus is an important connection to his own identity politics. This poem becomes a work about being a "foreigner" within U.S. society; it does not expound a particular statement about Mexican culture. Kerouac here is writing *to* home, but in this poem we get a very new glimpse of Kerouac and his "Americanness." He is not merely seeking a new literary and cultural space as an exile, but rather Kerouac engages once again in a dialectical relationship with his own country which, as the following observations makes clear, was as complex as its own contradictions.

> To decide without search that there was no important culture in the fifties, or that the genuine voice to be heard then was Nixon's whine, is to misunderstand the resilient nature of human culture in overcoming adversity. Indeed, a considerable part of fifties culture takes that point as its topic, emphasizing its resolute, dialectical relationship to the mainstream.... Fifties culture was an oppositional culture [Lhamon 28].

To locate resiliency within human culture is to recognize Kerouac's investment in literature, as a collection of voices forming a literal chorus. In the "12th Chorus," Kerouac is in Mexico and writing about Mexico but cannot escape from thoughts of his home. He is not so much "overcoming adversity" as denying its centrality in his own discourse; Kerouac returns to his childhood and to his "squeaks" that contain personal pleasure and innocence.

Traveling through Mexico City, Kerouac empowers himself as a poet, a Catholic, a Buddhist, a reborn Catholic and an American citizen. Each of these identities inform the major themes in the choruses as they appear, in general, almost randomly. That the emergence of the major themes appear in this way is not to say that the entire structure of *Mexico City Blues* is random and arbitrary. Indeed Michael Powell points out: "The seeming disparate 'choruses' are threaded not at random, but by a 'train of remembered experience....' The journey they sing defies daylight, and tunnels rhythmically from one seemingly inscrutable urban or musical 'confusion' to another" (2). Kerouac's journey in this poetry collection then, in short, "tunnels rhythmically." The theme of Mexico, like other major themes, appears with an indefinite probability of occurrence along such a journey.

In addition to the central theme of Mexico and Kerouac's self-conscious location in *Mexico City Blues*, Buddhism, music and children appear with a similarly indefinite probability of occurrence, reemerging sometimes expectedly and sometimes unexpectedly. "As

[Kerouac] says in the 36th Chorus of *Mexico City Blues,* the void is everywhere and the only direction to go is inward" (Hipkiss 51); this inwardness is structured, then, by Kerouac's look to associative thinking as one poetic model. As tropes, Buddhism and Mexico, for example, surface within the entire context of the poetry collection at spontaneous points, giving the overall effect of text and context the quality of something intracyclical. After the "12th Chorus" Mexico as more than an oblique theme is not glimpsed again by the reader until the "116th Chorus." The final two choruses which I will look at after the 116th are the "134th Chorus" and the "222nd Chorus." Together with the "12th Chorus," they can be characterized as individually distinct textual sites where Kerouac appears to find Mexico outside of the realm of change; however, as each chorus begins to chart the inevitable emergence of polyvocality in language, Kerouac pulls back and reverts to a dialectic of counterhegemonic investigation. Kerouac chooses to reenter the oppositional dialectics of 1950s literature rather than fully explore where the polyvocality could lead him. Thus, as a trope, Mexico is reiterated throughout these four choruses, but in a manner that returns the reader to the various intersections of Kerouac's American identity.

The phrase "a contrapuntal unity, not linear but reiterative"— expressed by Roberto González Echevarría in his critical study of the Latino author Alejo Carpentier (137)—seems perfectly applicable to what I term the "major Mexican choruses," which could conceivably be applicable to any of the themes in this work as they all appear, generally, unexpectedly and non-contiguously in an indefinite probability of occurrence. Reiteration here does not necessarily mean repetition, for aspects of Mexico and America are reconfigured in new and various ways without necessarily being identical sites of identification or contestation. These themes and the theme of Mexico specifically, as I have stated, are multivalent, and their multiple meanings frequently emerge from word play and particularly sound play.

Such sound play Kerouac hears in the songs of the Mexican children in the "12th Chorus," and he reiterates that sense in both the 116th and the 134th choruses that emphasizes the improvisational and informational.

This notion of improvisation informs the language of Kerouac's writing at an exact technical level. Though Kerouac had neither the knowledge of a musician nor the critical vocabulary of a person learned in the subject of music, he clearly demonstrates a profound identification of the creation of music with that of literary works [Weinreich 8–9].

This "creation of music" in Kerouac's hands seems to logically emerge from childhood and nonsense songs, a source which the author repeatedly draws upon to inform his mature, improvisational writing style so deeply immersed in his sense of jazz and its forms. The children's songs do not have to make explicit meaning, but are the articulation of innocence and discovery. Children along with minorities and other disempowered groups embodied an essential wisdom: "American society, Kerouac says, desperately needs an infusion of the qualities embodied by her oppressed minorities: the existential joy, wisdom, and nobility that comes from suffering and victimization" (Panish 107). Here it may be safe to speculate that Kerouac privileges the writer's position in defining what is joy, wisdom and nobility for society; in his schema, the musician is as important as the music.

The children of the "116th Chorus" are presented in relationship to Kerouac's own powers of visual and aural observation. The chorus begins with an ascription to American Jews who seem to be authors of the following song: "Niki Niki Niki-la / Che wa miena / Pee tee Wah" (*ll.* 2–4). The confusion as to authorship has to do with Kerouac's investment in jumping from idea to idea, for immediately the "Lil Mexico Children" (*l.* 5) are singing "Kitchi Kitchi / Kitchy val" (*ll.* 6–7). In either case language, as an agreed upon commodity of communication, yields to the secret music of its sound.

In this chorus particularly, Kerouac seems positioned as an observer in a bar, watching businessmen drink beer while he sits in a corner of "Bar's Alive" (*l.* 11) feeling like "old Canuck Pot" (*l.* 12). Evidently there is music in the background, or else it comes on to drown out the children's song; here that music could be a "Jolson" tune, a "Miles" tune or just his own Mexico City blues' song, but one characterized as remote, distant, as something that comes over "an Aztec Radio" (*l.* 16):

> with the sounds thick & guttural
> kicking out the teeth
> The Great Jazz Singer
> was Jolson the Vaudeville Singer?
> No, and not Miles, me.   [*ll.* 17–21]

Here Al Jolson, Miles Davis and Jack Kerouac are all presented as possible jazz singers; however, this "old Canuck pot" appears to emerge from that trio as "The Great Jazz Singer" (*l.* 19). Kerouac, the French Canadian, forms part of the trinity of a Jewish singer and an African-American jazz musician, but even these perennial outsiders are not as great as he is within the context of this chorus.

Mexico City Blues is a project that Kerouac envisions might include the musicality of all the "other" American jazz musicians and jazz singers, almost a repository of marginalized voices negotiated through him as poet. Jason Berry, Jonathan Foose and Tad Jones, in *Up from the Cradle of Jazz*, remind us: "Culturally, the most revolutionary change of the fifties was the embrace of traditionally black music by youngsters from the white middle class" (93). This project was primary to Kerouac, and this chorus, as well as the emergence of Charlie Parker in the later choruses, clearly locates that distinction. "In *Mexico City Blues* Charlie Parker, the great horn player, is said to be as musically important as Beethoven (Choruses 239–41)" (Hipkiss 35). I suggest this is so because like the music coming over the "Aztec Radio" in the "116th Chorus," Parker's music is made up of "sounds thick & gutteral / kicking out the teeth" (*ll.* 17–18). To deploy "a contrapuntal unity, not linear but reiterative" is to make music with its own interior logic, beauty and necessity.

The songs of the Mexican children reappear eighteen choruses later, in the next major Mexican chorus — the 134th. In this chorus it is not clear if the narrator is still in the bar, but clearly he is observing the children again. Kerouac does locate the time as "after dinner" (*l.* 5), so it could still be the bar scene with the children playing out on the street; once again, information and specifics are not as important as the visceral experience. In this chorus, the children yell: "Mo perro,

/ Mo perro, mo perro" (*ll.* 8–9). Here although "perro" likely means "dog," it is not clear what "mo" could mean, which inevitably returns this passage to the site of sound games. Kerouac hears the children say "mo perro," but its sense cannot be translocated in literal meaning because there is no Spanish word for "mo," although he may be hearing "mi" which means "my." "Mo" combined with the word "perro" rhymes, and it is also more assonant, more musical.

Juxtaposed against the noise of "Russian Spy Buses" (*l.* 14) which "[toot] Salud" (*ll.* 15–16) is the youthful exuberance of the children possibly looking for their dog or chasing a dog, the locals as subjects of study for foreigners in motion. Kerouac seems to be still and reflective but his mind is very much in motion; he takes the sound of the horn of the tour bus as an imperative to "Be healthy!" (or "Bottoms up!" if he is indeed still in the bar). Kerouac is in mellow spirit as he watches the dusk approach: "And the sky is purple / In old hazish Mexico / of Hashisch, Shaslik / And Veal Parmezan" (*ll.* 10–13). Certainly these lines reinforce the idea that it is dinner time, and Kerouac's mood is characterized as comparable to a drug-induced high.

Morphine constitutes a theme in the first four lines of this chorus:

> "The only cure for
>
> morphine poisoning
>
> Is more morphine."
>
> This is the real morphine.   [*ll.* 1–4]

Here it seems apparent that Kerouac has achieved a sense of peace with what he views around him, but this hustle and bustle is not distinctively Mexican. The peace within this poem is a peace he seems to have made within himself because he has made Mexico in his preconceived image, which is "a country where greatness reigned; where old men wore jeans and smoked on front porches and no one passed judgement on anyone else" (S. Turner 115). When Kerouac refers to "the real morphine" (*l.* 4), he may be talking about his version of the world around him.

What goes on around him in this chorus, as in other choruses, are sounds, activities and smells, but they are constantly mediated from a variety of sources. They emanate from "an Aztec Radio" or a "Mexico Camera," which opens up the "222nd Chorus," the next major Mexican chorus. There is a distance between the poet and the Mexico which he physically inhabits, a distance that allows him to rewrite, reclaim and reinscribe this foreign land with his own ideological priorities. In short, the narrator experiences peace despite where he is; Kerouac seemingly has found escape from his liminal restlessness.

Even some of his contemporaries were aware that here was a writer without the art of decentering himself. In the book *Heart Beat*, Carolyn Cassady elaborates on this characteristic of Kerouac's nature:

> [Jack] was far too moody, his feelings too touchy, too wrapped up in himself. This 'self' consciousness might be just the thing that made him a good writer. He could observe and report with brilliant clarity all the teeming life around him, but his efforts to partake of it and lose himself in it were generally disappointing [87].

In not losing himself, Kerouac remains in control of his writing and his environment. The experience of Mexico, then, as an actual place is reduced to little more than a postcard with smells and sounds. And postcards, we know, are as much about the egocentric notes attached to their backs as they are about the colorful, but flattened, images on their fronts. Part of the romance of the "premodern" is the precept of the primitive, the naïve, in the world; indeed, Jon Panish reminds us that the "white writers of the 1950s ... do not see the 'other' ... for what he or she is — a person just like any other who is involved in the complex relations of his or her culture — but as a static, unreal image" (108). This "static, unreal image" is indeed very postcard-like. While it is not Kerouac's project to present an "authentic" Mexico, it is astonishing that so little of this country permeates or reverberates throughout the choruses and how little everyday realities and complexities show through, again his "illusions of black and white blend and are negated by brown" (McCampbell Grace 113) in Mexico, thus making it a utopian society.

Although the metaphor of postcards seems apt here, it is important not to dismiss the choruses as static, for movement, physical and psychological, is both subject and form of these choruses. Critics have long investigated the road as trope in Kerouac's writing; interestingly, Powell takes this into the realm of railroad travel: "The Kerouacian odyssey is typically one of continuous and highly developed locomotion" (1). He refers to *Mexico City Blues* as a "frenetic rhapsodic train of choruses" (Powell 3). The peace found in the "134th Chorus" is temporary; Kerouac's restlessness, as evidenced in the other choruses, does not allow him to see Mexico as anything more than a site of departure or arrival.

The last major Mexican chorus opens with the image of "Mexico Camera" (*l.* 1). Here the narrator does not appear to be inactive; he walks "down Orizaba Street / looking everywhere" (*ll.* 2–3), but still he is an observer more than a participant. Indeed the narrator pulls back from the first-person perspective to a more detached, omniscient perspective as the "I" in this poem vanishes after line three. What the reader comes to see is excess in the form of "a mansion, with wall, big / lawn, Spanish interiors, fancy / windows very impressive" (*ll.* 4–6) which he characterizes amusingly as "Further bloated copulated bloats" (*l.* 7). This bourgeois overindulgence smacks of the 3rd chorus's warning about the climbing U.S. debt; in that poem, Kerouac admonishes the United States to attend to its debt(s), almost as if Kerouac is making the appeal on behalf of Mexico. Now here, in this chorus, we have a Mexico in which mansions locate a wealth that is as "bloated" as any estate in the First World.

Either the Mexican bourgeoisie is characterized as "Silent separative furniture" (*l.* 8) or the Mexicans and Indians who do not live in such opulence are characterized as such; the notion of separation as a division between the "haves" and the "have-nots" is demarcated here. Possession of material goods seem to follow the historical division of wealth: the Spanish mansion versus the masses. This connects to the "103rd Chorus" of *Mexico City Blues* where his father, according to Robert Hipkiss, is described as a person who "escaped knowing the meaninglessness of his existence, however, by playing the game American society plays, the competitive games of business and money-grubbing" (17–18). Indeed, it has been well documented that Kerouac was interested in class divisions and that "Jack saw the Mexicans as the 'fellaheen', the poor of the world: the people whom Oswald Spengler had identified in *The Decline of the West* as those who would inherit the Earth when the great powers had obliterated each other" (S. Turner 115). Gifford expounds upon Kerouac's notion of the fellaheen: "Jack's *fellaheen* were not the *grundrisse* of theoretical Marxism or the Third World of present-day politics, but simply the bulk of the planet's people, conducting their lives oblivious to the machinations of mainstream culture and power that functioned so well without their help" (231). Aside from the romantic view of the poor masses as outside of culture and power, certainly Kerouac's acknowledging of class structures is not the same as challenging them (in his writing, at the very least), as the curious lack of political anger or propaganda in this chorus makes obvious.

Here in *Mexico City Blues* as in "much of Beat writing, minorities are depicted as an enduring source of 'primitive' values whose identities remain stable and static" (Lardas 20). This seems particularly apt for this chorus, which seems to flatten reality upon a movie screen. In this chorus, Kerouac foregrounds "The Story of No-Mad, silent / separative corpses" (*ll.* 9–10) — and here it would seem likely to a reader that the masses fit into this story of his fellaheen "Nomad(s)." In Kerouac's gaze, the restlessness of the nomads becomes idealized or romanticized.

> The tropes and categories through which we view primitive societies draw lines and establish relations of power between us and them even as they presuppose that they mirror us.... For Euro-Americans, then, to study the primitive brings us always back to ourselves, which we reveal in the act of defining the Other [Torgovnick 11].

Kerouac is not so much invested in the political, cultural or historical Mexico that exists all about him, but, rather, he is seeking a means to return to himself. The poet sees the material manifestations of difference — as located in class, race and sometimes gender — without the ability to put other people's politicized realities before his own. Earlier Carolyn Cassady astutely stated that Kerouac was "too wrapped up in himself [and his] self consciousness"; furthermore, "his efforts to partake of [life around him] and lose himself in it were generally disappointing" (87). This particular chorus reinforces how comfortable Kerouac is in the former, passive role.

From the "Story of No-Mad" (*l.* 9) forward in this poem, we get several lines which name people either fictional or real ("Ignorino the Indian General" (*l.* 10), "Asserfelter Shnard Marade, / the Marauding Hightailer" (*ll.* 16–17) and "kierke / gaard" (*ll.* 19–20)), but generally as the chorus proceeds it once again breaks down into language games. The language games in this chorus, the last major Mexican chorus, end with the almost nonsensical couplet of "and bas bah / the Plap," as if this is yet another member of the cast of characters which includes Ignorino, the Marauding Marade and Kierkegaard. Generally these proper names appear but Kerouac does not do much with them; it is almost as if they are the final credits rolling at the end of a film whose subject was the profound gap between the rich and the poor. Once again, the poet is the one able to view both positions, as if he is a camera (which is not, itself, responsible for what is gazed upon).

To return to the first line of this particular chorus, the "Mexican Camera" he speaks of, then, is not a tourist's camera but a motion picture camera. Who may be behind the camera here? It seems unlikely that Kerouac is filming his movements in Mexico City. Also it is unlikely that a camera is filming him "walkin [sic] down Orizaba Street" (*l.* 2) as if he is in a movie, for this chorus contains details that would be unknown to a filmic character. Indeed, it is the view of a director or a writer or someone else entirely outside of the film who can see its overall structure, someone very much like an omniscient narrator in fiction.

Most likely, Kerouac is a spectator in a movie theatre and the movie he is watching almost gives him the sense that he is in it. This third scenario, then, seems the most likely; Kerouac is viewing a film and reporting on what he sees. This final potential scenario is also the most passive of the possibilities. Actually, at this moment in the choruses, Kerouac has rejected any attempt to participate in the Mexican experience and has taken refuge in a movie theater. Here he allows a film, presumably a Mexican film, to show him Mexico. Kerouac has consented to allow Mexico to be displayed for him, akin to the same manner that all the world is displayed for any American with often pedestrian motivations in the twentieth century: through film, through the director's gaze.

Mexico becomes emptied of meaning outside of the film for it becomes a referential within film's generic demands rather than the Mexico outside of the camera. Finally, then, Kerouac could just as easily be back in the U.S. gazing at this Mexico which has been reduced to the price of a movie ticket; and Kerouac, as rebellious Beat "activist," has reverted back to the position of a typical American moviegoer (much like any other passive tourist), a position which he does not avoid or resist. Finally it is inevitable that the reader notes how the structure of this last, major Mexican chorus pulls back from investigating polyvocality and returns us to the controlled borders of a director's gaze. Film fiction, like fictive poetry, is removed from the documentary process that can link viewer/reader with the subject in a manner that appears less "subjective," less relegated to the narrator's gaze, which is a project that Denise Levertov and Robert Hayden uniquely advance. A Hollywood film is not invested in accuracy, but rather in the nostalgia of (its own) constructed realities and their reifications.

Nicosia states that "empty" is one "of the key words in *Mexico City Blues*" (483), but that word does not appear in any of the four, major Mexican choruses. Not surprisingly the word "Mexico" appears the most often throughout the four choruses; it appears once in each of the poems and the word "Aztec" appears in two of them. In these four, major Mexican choruses, there is a significant lack of emptiness or silence, for Kerouac fills it up with the key concept of sound: the word "music" appears twice; the word "singer" appears twice; the verb "sings" appears once; and, finally, the word "song(s)" appears three times. Here it seems obvious that music and sounds animate Kerouac's Mexican choruses in much the way that Bakhtin said that "in the process of literary creation, languages interanimate each other and objectify precisely that side of one's own (and of the other's) language *that pertains to its world view*, its inner form, the axiologically accentuated system inherent in it" ("From the Prehistory" 62). Kerouac seems to conclude that inherent in the system of Mexico, however conflated and monolithic he sometimes presents it as, is musicality and spontaneous tonality, which he tries to recreate throughout the choruses.

Here in the "222nd Chorus," the adolescent sites of word play and polyvocality are, however, surprisingly absent. "Children" and "kids" were mentioned repeatedly in the other major Mexican choruses, but not in this last one; associated with children is Kerouac's liberal use of "little" or "Lil" in the major Mexican choruses, but again, here they are absent. This final, major Mexican chorus then seems somewhat distinct from the others in that it pulls away from the Bakhtinian notion of "verbal-ideological center" ("From the Prehistory" 48) in adolescent word play and sing-song and into a more contested space, a move which may be attributable to this chorus's position as following the central crisis of the book's philosophical inquiry. A sense of crisis, many critics and readers have pointed out, is central to Kerouac's works.

In the documentary *What Happened to Jack Kerouac?* McClure states: "Jack is a great visionary artist and each poem has to be a crisis, I mean, each novel, well, each poem too, *Mexico City Blues* for instance." This may be a slip of the tongue in regard to the poems, but it reveals some careful thought behind it. Nicosia might agree with McClure, but interestingly in terms of the overall structure of the poetry collection Nicosia points out that there is one, central crisis, which "occurs in choruses 194–197 [where Kerouac] is caught up like everyone else in an imaginary race, and the techniques he himself receives are from equally frantic participants" (485); this crisis, according to Nicosia, peaks in the "197th Chorus" with "a major turning away from Buddhism" (487). Thus, the "222nd Chorus" can be read as following Kerouac's retreat back to Catholicism, and similarly, Kerouac's internal desire to retreat back to the United States.

After the "222nd Chorus" Mexico only shows up in a superficial way in the "224th Chorus" to describe the quality of a "keener / and moaner" (*ll.* 4–5) as having the intensity of a mourner in a "Mexican Funeral home" (*l.* 6). From this point through the last eighteen choruses, Mexico disappears entirely. Buddhism as a major theme reappears and then shortly after, Charlie Parker and jazz come to dominate as *Mexico City Blues* arrives at a "conclusion." The final chorus, the

"242nd Chorus," offers us a key to the entire collection of Kerouac's poems. He states: "The sound in your mind / is the first sound / that you could sing" (*ll.* 1–3), a disembodied voice, a sound "in [the] mind" (*l.* 1), as well as a song of himself. This not only returns us to the sense that meanings in these choruses reside in sounds and sound play, but that the children's songs in the earlier major Mexican choruses play a pivotal role. The jazz musician, the poet and the singing children trust the sound of language to contain the meaning of language.

The last two lines in *Mexico City Blues* are: "All's well! / I am the Guard" (*ll.* 23–24). Note here that Kerouac is neither a peace keeper nor an agent of civil disobedience; he is merely a "Guard," which seems to be the very role the United States wants to play with its neighbors to the immediate south throughout the twentieth century. Interestingly, Kerouac redefines that guardian-like role so that order is not only maintained but its guardian-like function is made an active force which exerts control over chaos. This is demonstrated in the line preceding the penultimate line of the "242nd Chorus" where Kerouac as narrator orders: "Stop the murder and the suicide!" (*l.* 22), before he announces that "All's well!" Here he does not command Mexico or the United States to stop the killing but seemingly he orders death in the form of "that grim reper [sic]" (*l.* 7) to "Stop the murder and the suicide!" (*l.* 22). At the end of *Mexico City Blues* Kerouac is disembodied, becoming a voice, a sound "in [the] mind" (*l.* 1) and a song of himself, simultaneously.

Kerouac's *Mexico City Blues* is a complex manuscript about location and dislocation. His links to a French-Canadian culture allow Kerouac to better understand the position of the outsider, his sense of questioning where be belonged in this world (Wilson 89); Kerouac, the observer, takes very little for granted but finds mostly emotional and intellectual pleasure in exploration of the self rather than exploration of Mexico, its people and its culture(s). This poetry collection has been viewed mainly as a Buddhist meditation, but it is much more, for the poems reconfirm Kerouac's American citizenship. McClure insists that "Kerouac's epic is a poem outside history, a record of discrete illuminations in the present" (Foster 43), but to relegate this writer and other Beat writers outside of history is to misunderstand the contextual forces which shape their *oeuvre*.

Polyvocality is a recognition of multiple voices speaking of multiple things simultaneously which may mean that there are some specific words and phrases which are mis-heard or not heard at all. Kerouac is sensitive to the sound of language as evidenced in his many references to singing children and to the nonsensical (to him) Spanish language all about him. He fails to imagine that Mexicans and Mexican Indians in their own country and speaking their own language(s) might open up new discursive practices (how people talk and write about themselves and others) in which Kerouac is truly decentered, but which may ultimately offer him new ways of seeing. Here, the author is centered; he is the one opening up and, importantly, controlling these blues' choruses; interestingly, the "phrase 'the blues' is derived from 'the blue devils,' a mental affliction of the early nineteenth century defined by the OED as despondency or spiritual depression" (Davis 243). Generally, these are not the blues *of* Mexico so much as they are Kerouac's blues *to* America.

Bakhtin suggests that "we find a rich world of diverse forms that transmit, mimic and represent from various vantage points another's word, another's speech and language" ("From the Prehistory" 50). The Mexico in *Mexico City Blues* contains a potentiality for interaction, a potentiality that is not always realized. This is partly due to the Buddhist notion of letting go of the actual world that may prove to be only an illusion after all; the specific yields to the abstract. Meditation inevitably leads Kerouac to rethink his childhood and other autobiographical moments which now exist as memories turned into words.

Music becomes the conduit between memory and words but not the music of the mainstream culture. When the "Beats could not connect with white fathers — symbolically, when orthodox mentors proved inadequate — they adopted black jazzlore.... [Kerouac's] mind's tinsmith is a fantasy of derelict and black culture compacted into a blues ethic" (Lhamon 70). This "black jazzlore" becomes the very language of Kerouac's own exile, search for home, and his intertwining personal discourse with public discourse. Here Emily Martin in "Body Narratives, Body Boundaries" reminds us that Foucault states that "modern forms of power are not repressive, but productive. They do not just deny, prohibit, repress, and restrict; more importantly, they produce discourses, knowledge, pleasures, and goods" (409). In other words, Kerouac deploys the pleasure of language, as located in sound and meaning, as a productive, creative strategy.

This production is what Bakhtin has named "interillumination" ("From the Prehistory" 49), that is, the intertextuality inherent in or created between disparate moments of knowledge. For Kerouac, word and language play and the spaces that open up for him between such language play and its meaning(s) are, indeed, almost essential illuminations, and Nicosia reminds us that to Kerouac "light-in-darkness usually suggests home, warmth, and shelter, often beyond the wanderer's reach" (313). Bakhtin's "interillumination" demands complex readings of multi-layered texts, a demand equally challenging to the writer and to the reader. While home may be "beyond the wanderer's reach," the words and music that articulate the past are at hand.

There have been important studies in which Kerouac has been placed within his own autobiographical contexts, spaces that need to be reconsidered. It is important to remember that

> After Lowell, the next most frequent setting, especially early in the book, is Mexico City, suggesting the importance in his subconscious of this one foreign place to which he became attached over New York and San Francisco, with which he had much stronger and longer connections. Mexico City, however, was "abroad" for Kerouac, the furthest place from Lowell for which he developed any real feelings though also the site of such disastrous experiences as Neal's desertion and the sad affair with Tristessa [French 100].

This passage offers specific coordinates to Kerouac's life, but it is perhaps too linear an explanation. *Mexico City Blues* insists that all these locations exist simultaneously within the jazzlore structure; Kerouac is sure they can encompass even his own contradictions.

Polyvocality accommodates contradiction and chaos, which Kerouac strives to achieve but ultimately fails at in *Mexico City Blues*. According to Bakhtin, "After all, it is possible to objectivize one's own particular language, its internal form, the peculiarities of its world view, its specific linguistic habits, only in the light of another language belonging to someone else, which is almost as much 'one's own' as one's native language" ("From the Prehistory" 62). While this strategy is possible, it does not come to fruition in Kerouac's choruses; these poems return to a dialectical space in which Kerouac reifies his position as an outsider, as merely a protester on the margins of American mainstream culture.

This position as an outsider, a protester on the margins, is a role that becomes disempowered by the power structure of the decade; Kerouac, then, is forced into a role — or places himself in a role — that is, ultimately, infantalized. It is agreed that

> Mid-century America was a country of families: Father, Mother, and the children, watching television programs about fathers, mothers, and children.... Eisenhower, the general who had prosecuted the hot war, spoke to his constituents in a slow and patient manner, explaining the necessity for the arms race and the bomb shelters in the way a grandfather might explain a frightening noise in the night to a child [Gifford 231].

This explanation reveals the exact site where the patriarchal discourse is transferred over to the next generation. Kerouac's personal actions and public texts were often dismissed as immature writing, one way to dismiss "formlessness" in order to detonate content. The following comment sums up the overall critical reception of *Mexico City Blues*: "Kerouac's poetry has been universally damned by his reviewers because of its sloppiness and vacuity" (Hipkiss 80). It would be an interesting project to look at these "damnations" in light of recent critical work on the interstices of class and race. What may be behind these dismissals is the racist need for white America to empty African-American culture (and other minority cultures) of the potentiality to produce "discourses, knowledge, pleasures" (Martin 409) etc. outside of the realm of hegemonic controls. Kerouac's voluntary allegiance or self-modeling after African-American jazz forms can be viewed as one of the seeds of greater social revolution which did come to pass later in the 1960s.

The Other is typically infantalized as a means to keep their participation at bay or, at the very least, to force him/her/them into a dialogue of unequals. Kerouac foregrounds this inequality without always having been aware of his own complicity. It is interesting that the outsiders and the children seem to exist as a necessary category for Kerouac and his critics. Note the following statement's marginalization and dismissal of the Other: "the artist keeps alive the memories of childhood, embellishes them.... [Kerouac's] embellishment takes the form of an extension of the child's vision to the lives of unsophisticated primitives" (Hipkiss 13). This simplification of Kerouac's writing belies the complicated replication of social institutions, practices and discourses in these meditations.

Mexico City Blues is indeed a text of polyvocality but of one whose agency for change or critique is limited in scope and success. Although there may be "no simple relationship between what is directly seen and what is signified" (Urry 146), this may be lost on Kerouac. Partly, this could be due to his reluctant acceptance of his prescribed role as outsider. By failing to fully address his own real marginalization as a French Canadian, Kerouac divides American culture into two overly simplistic categories, the mainstream and those who oppose the mainstream. He assumed that the latter position was truly one category instead of being many categories. In assuming an intimate relationship with the Other — such as Mexicans, Mexican Indians, African Americans, etc. — he ironically erases the differences between groups, again reproducing the assumptions of our nation's exceptionalism (Lardas 111).

Kerouac writes in a December 3, 1950, letter to Neal Cassady: "Now you can see why my thoughts turn to Mexico; if I can land a little job with some American company I can stay there the rest of my life" (*Selected Letters* 240). This wish is never realized, for Kerouac returns to the United States and eventually achieves the fame he always craved; Kerouac's writing becomes co-opted by patriarchal power in which the outsider is no longer resisted but appropriated. "*Mexico City Blues*, at last, resolves itself into a special silence, a silence that recalls to us that the poet's medium is just a finger pointing in the right direction" (Jones 183). In actuality, this "special silence" is the shutting down of polyvocality, and all that is left to Kerouac is the physicality innate in language. The silence, then, can be read less as voluntary than as accepted after a long period of resistance; the silenced ends up accepting the silence. Not unlike Dean Moriarty's thumb forced to be poised in the air near the end of *On the Road*, Kerouac is left silenced in Mexico with no new roads open to him so he merely, quietly, points *to* home, to America.

3

Gregory Corso

Gregory Corso, like many of the Beat writers, visited Mexico in the 1950s but barely wrote anything significant about that experience. In the two brief poems about his trip—"Mexican Impressions" and "Puma in Chapultepec Zoo"—Corso seems strangely alienated from the subject of Mexico. In Michael Skau's book, *"A Clown in a Grave": Complexities and Tensions in the Works of Gregory Corso,* he writes that often Corso's "fantasized projections of foreign locales butt up against an implacable reality" (23). It seems the reality here, for Corso, is that he does not want to immerse himself in the Mexican culture. Corso's experiences in Mexico and his "reporting" of these experiences in these two poems reveal that he is writing about America rather than writing about Mexico, and rather nostalgically at that.

Mexico does not exist as a full subject independent of Corso's own ideologies or as a worthy conversant. He writes *back* home from Mexico to the United States. The two poems, "Mexican Impressions" and "Puma in Chapultepec Zoo," are directly engaged in notions of dislocation. The idea of "going foreign" during his trip to Mexico does not appeal to Corso. At least for this trip, Corso does not celebrate "the richness of the journey" as most Beats attempted to do (Lardas 170). Generally, foreignness is a somewhat attractive concept; it can be a desire for the experience that may lead to some sense of transcendence through the details of location. Corso looks at Mexico and is less than enthusiastic. Quickly it becomes clear to him and his readers that there will be no transcendence in Corso's experience(s) of

Mexico. He makes no attempt to come to terms with that which appears foreign, and he inevitably retreats into his own complex American identity. Corso is writing "back" home, that is, toward a United States that he has temporarily left behind and desires to return to in the near future because the present, specifically the present of Mexico, is emptied of any significant contribution to his own consciousness.

Corso fails to address the fact that "Mexico is a complex, violent, mysterious, ugly-beautiful reality, with its subterranean forces of Indian culture, and resentment, historical traumas and contradictory masks imposed or donned over the centuries" (Boldy 157). That his failure to do this is part of his overall project is emphasized by Gregory Stephenson in his article "'The Arcadian Map': Notes on the Poetry of Gregory Corso" in *The Daybreak Boys*: "though there are prisons in the world and in the mind, there are also towers" (79). Corso has several layers he can investigate here: the subterranean, the surface and the upward-reaching structures of hope. Corso chooses to construct a superficial impression of the landscape around him, both in his mind and his text, rather than actually observe and investigate the Mexico that is briefly a reality in front of him.

Interestingly, Corso's strategy to deal with his reactions to being "away" from the United States and dislocated is to center hegemonic "Americanness"; this centering, here, in Corso's work, can be defined as his need for instant comfort, familiarity and safe routine. There are many autobiographical reasons why this poet might prove vulnerable to flux, to change or to the work required to accommodate or embrace realities beyond individual control. When Corso came into [New York City] in 1953 he was twenty-three, dark-haired, short,

> with strong eyes and brooding good looks. He was Italian, born on Bleecker Street in the Village in New York, but his mother had died and his father had abandoned him. He'd spent most of his life in institutions or jail. He began writing poetry in prison, and he had been sitting in a Village bar just after his release in 1951 when Allen saw him and began talking with him. Gregory showed Allen some of his writing, and Allen enthusiastically admitted him into their small group [Charters 193].

3. Gregory Corso

One might anticipate the expectations of instant comfort, familiarity and safe routine, or hegemonic "Americanness" to be more problematized in Corso's work considering his working-class background and tough, street-wise adolescence (which connote counter-hegemonic characteristics); he doesn't seem to seek affiliation as much as appreciation.

The following quotation summarizes the context in which Corso and his colleagues wrote: "It was a mean time. The nation was ready for witch-hunts. We had come out of World War Two stronger and more powerful and more affluent than ever before, but the rest of the world, alien and unsettling, seemed to press closer now than many Americans wanted it to" (Halberstam 9). Corso's outsider position, from rebel youth to Beat protégé, helped him understand that these witch hunts had profound ideological and political implications exactly because it "was a mean time." The Beats particularly recognized that U.S. hegemony found not only "the rest of the world" alien and unsettling but anything outside of its own mainstream "alien and unsettling."

Corso's poems, "Mexican Impressions" and "Puma in Chapultepec Zoo," make no serious attempt to contradict anything "alien and unsettling"; indeed, it becomes obvious that Corso is making no attempt to "lose himself" in Mexico. Even though a "gaze is after all visual, it can literally take a split second" (Urry 42), and for Corso "a split second" seems sufficient. In fact, on his brief trip to Guadalajara in the autumn of 1956 with Allen Ginsberg, Peter Orlovsky and his brother en route to visit Denise Levertov and her husband Mitchell Goodman, Corso looks at and records only brief glimpses of death and doom in Mexico, elements which come to permeate the poems from *Gasoline*. Mark Doty states that "*Gasoline* (1958) gathered exuberant, frequently comic poems held together by the vividness of the speaker's voice, an enthusiastic, energetic tone which rushes along declaiming jokes, condemnations, and praises" (144–45). Yet, Corso's "comic" nature in poetry, noticeably, plays little part in either "Mexican Impressions" or "Puma in Chapultepec Zoo," which suggests there may be a cultural and literary anxiety present here, the foreign geography too serious of a threshing ground. Stephenson succinctly states: "For Corso, the poet and the clown are one, engaged in the ultimate struggle of desire against death, vision against objective, external reality" ("'The

Arcadian Map'" 77). The comic stance is not foregrounded in "Mexican Impressions," replaced instead by a tourist's gaze from a moving car, observation privileged over the intimacy required of humans at all levels.

One of the key framing techniques of the five-part, twenty-seven-line poem "Mexican Impressions" occurs not only in the first section but in the very first two lines of the poem sequence. Corso writes, "Through a moving window / I see a glimpse...." Here it is quite clear that Corso is more invested in separation than in linkages; he chooses to remain in a moving automobile and simply "glimpse" what passes, by happenstance. Interestingly the details are twice removed; Corso does not state that he "sees" but that he "see[s] a glimpse" (*l.* 2). Those things which he sees are: "burros / a Pepsi Cola stand, / [and] an old Indian sitting / smiling toothless by a hut" (*ll.* 2–5). Corso's "quest" is for a momentary present filled with vivid details presented through detached observations, instead of an attempt to "[gain] a new perspective on the values of the dominant culture [the United States]" (Lardas 169). Here Bakhtin's postulations are applicable to Corso, considering that "when the present becomes the center of human orientation in time and in the world, time and world lose their completeness as a whole as well as in each of their parts" ("Epic and Novel" 30); this seems particularly apt. Corso's poem reveals an "impersonal" Mexico that the poet-narrator experiences through incidental details; ultimately, however, they are glimpses observed, impressions quite removed from direct experience. Indeed, they are observations glimpsed from a moving automobile and are, thus, very myopic, incomplete.

Two of the things which Corso looks at from the "moving window" would seem to be things a typical "foreigner" would expect to see, burros and "an old Indian ... by a hut" (*ll.* 4–5). That the old Indian is toothless connotes the lack of hope present in Mexico, which Corso expounds upon elsewhere in this poem sequence. Corso also sees "a Pepsi Cola stand" (*l.* 3). Corso emphasizes poverty, even as capitalism, through the signifier of the soda pop, has clearly made its inroads into to this rural location; here is a poet aware of contradictions. For a moment, Pepsi Cola is a bridge to Corso's own cultural identity, but any associated strategies that may be at play here are simply not developed. The stand of soda pop is not pulled out of its context from other mere "Mexican" details. It stands as dull and as ahistorical as the burros and the old Indian. Urry's observation that the "typical tourist experience is anyway to see *named* scenes through a *frame*, such as the hotel window, the car windscreen or the window of the coach" (90–91) is particularly apt here. Corso, as poet-narrator, remains inside his car, looking at Mexico pass from the highway, disassociated from the political implications of either poverty, capitalism or any other characteristics to be found in Mexico.

In this section of "Mexican Impressions," Corso not only seems reluctant to immerse himself in the culture but takes comfort in his tourist-like position as he fails to evaluate the details which pass by. We know that the old Indian is a mere curiosity because he is mentioned, but he is not elaborated upon. That he is toothless seems one more scrap of detail rather than any sort of an analysis of an economic system that oppresses the many. Corso fails to maintain a "living contact with unfinished, still evolving contemporary reality" which Bakhtin terms "the openended present" ("Epic and Novel" 7). There is, for Corso, no explanation of the juxtaposition of Mexico and Pepsi Cola; the narrative implied by history and cultural contact is absent. In all likelihood, the reader senses that the old Indian's "toothlessness" is a synecdoche for his suffering, but in Corso's flat, unevaluative poetic manner here it seems almost unimportant, a psychic souvenir. This implicates Corso in the project of American ethnocentric gazing at the Other, the foreign, which fails to challenge "strictly binary formations" (Kaplan 20): the Other vs. the self, the global citizen vs. tourist.

In centralizing his own viewpoints as naturalized, Corso is just left with the narratives of individual tragedies and triumphs, reifying the self as the tourist in these particular poems. Interestingly, Stephenson writes that Corso's "work represents an attempt to redeem the human psyche from its fallen state, from its exile, and to restore it to true being" (*Exiled Angel* 7). There should be a question as to whether or not that redemption applies only to mainstream American citizens, for in "Mexican Impressions" there is an implied fatalism by which no one can be restored — particularly the toothless old Indian in this first section — not even by Corso as poet. The car continues its way through

Mexico without the writer attempting to redeem anything in the unfolding countryside before him.

Stephenson outlines Corso's overall poetic project as the following: "Out of the stricken landscape of our age, Corso has brought us a vision of Arcadia" (89). In his treatment of Mexico, Corso relegates "our age" or any historical age to the present. It is not a vision of Arcadia that he looks upon but a country with a "stricken landscape." Corso neither sees nor seeks the pastoral, and yet when he encounters the "third world" he is noticeably unable to accept it on its own terms (or its harsh realities when unfiltered, when not literary). "Vision," then, is a means to ahistoricize or depoliticize what is revealed to him from a moving car; movement itself allows Corso the luxury of observation without immediate political responsibilities or visceral contact.

The second section of "Mexican Impressions" begins when the poet is "Stopping at Guaymas" (*l.* 6); here Corso observes "a brand new Ford pick-up / filled with melancholy laborers" (*ll.* 7–8). There is an empathy with the laborers' "melancholy," but nothing occurs beyond the recognition of this empathy; labor is reduced to a mere fact of everyday life, rather than investigated within socioeconomic constructs. Evidently both the Ford pick-up, as well as the automobile Corso and his companions are driving in, stop at Guaymas. This particular location reveals little, except that as a town it is approximately 400 miles down Mexico's western coast from the border town of San Luis Rio Colorado. That Corso and his companions need to stop seems logical (to eat or relieve themselves), but it also underscores the beginning of Corso's literary reluctance to go deeper into Mexico, to move from the coastal highway into the interior.

More integral to this poem than Corso's geographical location is the fact that he and his companions are making stops, as well as the presence of the "young child" (*l.* 9) who Corso sees in the Ford pick-up. Without chatting with the child and without overhearing any particular conversation, Corso reduces the boy's fate — and we know it's a boy because of the possessive pronoun "his" in the following line — to one of doom, which seems to invert the Bakhtinian notion of an "openended present" ("Epic and Novel" 11) into one of a closed present. Corso, as poet-narrator, states that this young boy is "doomed by his sombrero" (*l.* 10). That the boy must be a child of one of the laborers becomes peripheral to the material presence of his "sombrero," which here functions less as a detail of the necessity to wear one in the agricultural fields in Mexico's climate than as a signifier for Mexico itself. The stereotypical sombrero (in Corso's view) reduces an individual, even a child, to a prescripted destiny. Corso doesn't question this; he doesn't even imagine any act of intervention. One of Marianna Torgovnick's observations in *Gone Primitive: Savage Intellects, Modern Lives* is useful here: "But cultural relativism needed time to really take hold since it challenged so strongly Western assumptions of superiority" (19). This characterization (a dismissal) of a child "doomed" to his fate speaks volumes of Corso's own privileged status, even though he imagines himself—and often is—an outsider. Here Corso's identity as an exotic and flamboyant bad boy, the owner of "a box of crazy toys" as Ginsberg characterizes him in the Introduction to *Gasoline* (7), cannot be reckoned with his continual desire for instant comfort, familiarity and safe routine.

Corso's detail of the "sombrero" emphasizes local color and tourist culture, for it is this particular type of hat that many tourists to Mexico find so exotically, organically and flamboyantly Mexican. Again, this detail underscores Corso's position in these poems as a tourist, making little attempt to immerse himself in the culture but feeling quite free to remark on or criticize the culture with superficial observations. Stephenson in his book *Exiled Angel* points out that in "the poems of *Gasoline* we encounter again the motif of predatory devouring and destruction of innocence and beauty, already familiar from Corso's first collection" (25), but that "destruction" here does not lead to any sense of hope or transcendence, which many critics point out is often central to Corso's works. Stephenson generalizes: "As in Corso's first collection, images of violence and death, especially the death of children, are frequent in the poems of *Gasoline* ... [including] the 'young child—doomed by his sombrero' who is glimpsed in 'Mexican Impressions'" (28). Although the boy is not necessarily "doomed" to an early death, perhaps on one level he might as well be, at least in Corso's mind. Once innocence and beauty are gone, according to this poet-narrator, what is there left to live for?

The sense of "destruction of innocence and beauty" seems inevitable in this section; the Mexican child is doomed simply by having been born Mexican and obviously poor. In turn, the gaze of the poet-narrator is unidirectional, for the laborer's son does not look back at Corso; in fact, he does not even register his presence, at least not within the poem. The Mexicans are present only in the gaze of the poet-narrator, and they neither speak nor act. They are characterized here as lacking agency, doomed by the country they were born into. Again this poem foregrounds a "closed present," in which implications of history, culture and everyday realities may be considered but their totalities, their complexities, are ignored.

Bakhtin reminds us that "when the present becomes the center of human orientation in time and in the world, time and world lose their completeness as a whole as well as in each of their parts" ("Epic and Novel" 30). Inevitably, this poem might as well be about a visit to a dude ranch for here, in section two of "Mexican Impressions," American ethnocentric hegemony remains centered, as it has been throughout the first ten lines of this poem sequence. This is not a poem about the Mexican culture or the experience of being between cultures but about Corso's connections to hegemonic American culture, which seems to fly in the face of his identity politics as the son of the working-class himself and as an adolescent/adult once imprisoned. Obvious connections between Corso's own life and childhood and the young boy's are not investigated, which some readers may lament as a missed opportunity.

The silences in this poem intrigue me, for Corso sifts through these laborers for the image of the boy in the driver's seat, a child forced into adulthood. It is as if Corso cannot focus too long on this moment for the section ends abruptly, "doom" taking over narrative. "Corso's poetic imagination is, then, essentially a rejection of the real" (Stephenson, "'The Arcadian Map'" 75) which sounds like a powerful summation, but it is also a damning one: Corso's rejection of the real also dismisses labor, agency, cultural difference (here signified as a sombrero, essentialism as a system). This is a poet who must invent, for what is real comes with costs he isn't prepared to pay.

The only people in the first section of this five-section poem sequence are the poet-narrator and "an old Indian" (*l.* 4), and in the second section the poet-narrator and his traveling companions are there, assumably, because their car makes a stop "at Guaymas" but the "young child" (*l.* 9) is the foregrounded individual. Beginning in the third section, and continuing to the end of this poem sequence, there is only the poet-narrator and the "things" that he sees; absence of people becomes a major and dominant characteristic here. There are no Mexicans, Mexican Indians or Mexican laborers' children; individuals, but for the poet, are absent from the poem and only Mexican objects are present (and presentable).

The first detail Corso observes in section three is not merely recorded but amplified upon by the poet-narrator. There is the image of a windmill rising from the wilds, an image which Corso immediately finds "incongruous" to Mexico and its landscape:

> Windmill, silverwooded, slatless, motionless in Mexico —
> Birdlike incongruous windmill, like a broken crane,
> One-legged, stiff, arbitrary, with wide watchful eye,
> How did you happen here? — All alone, alien, helpless,
> Here where there is no wind? [*ll.* 11–15]

Again, Corso reduces Mexico and its physicality to a smaller (or the smallest) detail, for he prefers to keep his gaze myopic and self-controlled. He does not see the beauty or the vastness of the landscape, either its sensual or destructive nature, but focuses upon one small, "doomed" thing as a synecdoche for the state that Mexico and its inhabitants are in. Stephenson writes: "Closely related to the violence-and-death motif in Corso's poetry are the recurring images of alienation and loss. The windmill 'alone, alien, helpless' among cacti in a windless land ... is one such figure..." (*Exiled Angel* 28). In this passage particularly, the "slatless" windmill is less a synecdoche for Mexico as a material metaphor than for something "alone, alien, helpless" (*l.* 14) in Mexico, which is ultimately the poet-narrator.

Corso identifies with this image that is "like a broken crane, / One-legged, stiff, arbitrary, with wide watchful eye ... alone, alien, helpless" (*ll.* 12–14). Outside of his own culture, Corso experiences the people and things stiffly, and his presence here (this trip) is the result of a random, illogical and impulsive decision. What he looks at in Mexico he looks at "with wide watchful eye," which is the gaze of a spectator who feels too "alien" to understand the spectacle at which he is gazing, much less to participate in it. Ultimately, the windmill becomes something of a transplanted monkish figure, someone assigned to this foreign land but not of it. Bakhtin observes that "one can relate to the past in a familiar way (as if relating to 'my' present), but in so doing we ignore the presentness of the present and the pastness of the past" ("Epic and Novel" 14). Corso imposes an alienation upon a land that he has little interest in. The windmill, a man-made structure, has an obvious European genealogy but now it's central to its own tragedy simply because of its "dislocation." Corso even makes the wind seem inattentive to this "incongruous" tower; the poet-narrator is opened, however briefly, to questioning his assumptions about Mexico and its landscape, even if done unconsciously. Then, the moment passes, a windmill without a wind being overwhelmingly unnatural.

In this same section, it is the cactus that signifies Mexico and "Mexicanness." Unlike the windmill, the cactus "outlives" (*l.* 18) the "gaunt structure" (*l.* 16) of the "birdlike" windmill. The poet-narrator addresses the "silverwooded" structure directly: "Living gaunt structure resigned, are you pleased / with this dry windless monkage?" (*ll.* 16–17). Corso is asking himself as well as the windmill — "How did [we] happen here?" (*l.* 14), which positions him outside of the culture, as if he were back in the United States. Of the windmill and himself, Corso is asking figuratively: Don't we wish we were *back* home? The poem, then, becomes a way to write himself back home, to that which is not foreign and alien, to a place where he does not feel helpless and resigned. "In fact, Corso often reveals a conservatism that ennobles the past — personally, nationally, and historically" (Skau 41). It is important to note that the cactus in the poem reintroduces the notion of the primitive, the world reduced to its prickly essential. Skau reminds us that such nostalgia involves "what Corso sees as the more innocent periods in human civilization, treasuring classicism and the noble savage of prerational, primitive culture" (6). Such nostalgia, inevitably, relies upon both disaffiliation and disengagement; the cactus, or the collective cacti, emphasizes a landscape not Corso's.

Once we reach this midway point in the poem sequence, it becomes very clear to the reader that disengagement is exactly what is going on here. Somewhere beyond Corso's immediate Mexican experiences, there are engagements for him; within this poem, it is clear that such emotional and intellectual investments are reserved for his return to the United States. There is ultimately a recognition that the cactus is a noble entity, for in its passivity it outlives human civilizations' best showcases. "Softer," writes Corso, and yet he has a hard heart, for he doesn't see a Mexico that is "alive" beyond this one cactus, a singularity bearing a mighty weight.

Corso's position at the center of American hegemony is nowhere more obvious than in the first line of the fourth section of the poem sequence: "I tell you, Mexico" (*l.* 19). For a short time, the poet-narrator moves from his stance as observer to a self-assumed position of authority. The key to Corso's shift is not evident until the last line of this section, which reads, revealingly, "[It] wrecks my equestrian dreams of nightmare" (*l.* 24). Because the reality of Mexico defies even this poet's nightmarish dreams of Mexico, because the "openended present" ("Bakhtin, "Epic and Novel" 11) dares to write itself upon Corso's palimpsest of closed, poetic visions of Mexico, Mexico is to be taken to task. Obviously a monologue is not a site of polyvocality.

Here Corso makes an attempt to admonish the country. Note that he neither specifically disapproves of the actions of the nation's political and religious leaders nor the actions of the corrupt regional bosses known as *caciques*. Instead he disapproves of Mexico in its entirety. Corso's monolithic, personified construct of Mexico is supposed to sit up and listen as he admonishes:

> I tell you, Mexico —
> I think miles and miles of dead full-bodied horses —
> Thoroughbreds and work horses, flat on their sides
> Stiffened with straight legs and lipless mouths.
> It is the stiff leg, Mexico, the jutted tooth,
> That wrecks my equestrian dreams of nightmare. [*ll.* 19–24]

Corso's tone, which could be characterized as almost horrific, is altruistic because of the almost didactic tone to "you, Mexico," which places him within the center of U.S. hegemony. Rather than critiquing the poverty, oppression and politics of the country, of which all the dead horses are surely a symptom, Corso self-righteously aligns himself with the historical imperialistic stance of the United States, particularly in the 1950s. Corso's use of the verb "wreck" is an accusation, a scolding of the romanticism he has brought along to his borrowed Mexico.

Seemingly such a heuristic position is not an anomaly to this poet. In his article about Corso, Stephenson reminds us:

> Concerning his conception of the role of the poet in the world, Corso has written: "Someone must 'Christopher-Columbus' the mind," the great expanse of consciousness, and this the poet does. But unlike Columbus who discovered a new world that was there, the poet must make a new world ["'The Arcadian Map'" 88–89].

Importantly, Mexico is real and doesn't necessarily have to be invented. This is an excellent example of Corso's disinterest in historicizing the world about him. In the fourth section of "Mexican Impressions," Corso is doing more than acting like someone who "must 'Christopher-Columbus' the mind"; indeed, Corso is acting like any global-variety conquistador. He acts out the role of American poet-hero who has more in common with the U.S. mainstream than with his Beat compatriots, a distant moralist astonished by the realities of humans and animals beyond or outside of Corso's cosmology.

Corso's comfortable position as decoder is one with profound links to the United States in the 1950s, and that continues through to today; there is the continual assumption that the United States's sheer power and wealth give it an imperative to police or manipulate the globe. The importance of the verb "wrecks" in line 24 cannot be minimized. The rotting horses disturb Corso's "dreams of nightmares" (*l.* 24), and he clearly resents the imposition of such reality into his writing (his life). There is a continuing sense that Corso in Mexico finds that any moment in which a "real" Mexico exists is an intrusion. It is interesting that Corso, an outsider in many ways, when outside of his own culture, is unaware that "national myth and national tradition ...

permeate this language" (Bakhtin, "From the Prehistory" 61). Corso focuses on "the jutted tooth" (*l.* 23) and never questions why this strikes him as unnatural.

Apparently, in this poem, Corso is writing himself back into mainstream space. By writing back home about the ultimate despair inherent in Mexico's political, social and cultural structure, Corso is truly rewriting himself into the heart of the American identity as it existed in the generally stifling conformist decade of the fifties. In ascribing the power to make "a discovery of correspondences and conjunctions, a reconciliation of opposites" (Stephenson, "'The Arcadian Map'" 76), Corso simply dismisses what cannot be reconciled within his world view: Mexico. Here, Mexico serves merely as a subject of objectification of his superficial observation. Ultimately, this "other country" appears humanly painful and dependent upon his myopic perspectives; the translator has gained greater importance than what is being translated.

"Explicit cognition is enjoined" are the words Richard Eberhart uses to emphasize the earliest evidences of the San Francisco poetry renaissance in his brief essay "West Coast Rhythms" (25). As a phrase, it seems to describe both the ultimate strophe of "Mexican Impressions," section five, and Corso's shorter but similar work "Puma in Chapultepec Zoo." After twenty-four lines of disengaged observation that always hints at a negative judgment of what Corso's come "to know" about Mexico, he states simply in the last three lines of "Mexican Impressions": "In the Mexican Zoo / they have ordinary / American cows" (*ll.* 25–27). Initially the short strophe may seem like brief detail and detached observation, but clearly there is a sense of admonition here which stems from disappointment and his hunger for valued adventure. Although many critics point to Corso's comic quality, which is definitely a layer here, this strophe, in the context of this sober poem sequence, contains more pathos (or even bathos) than hilarity.

To the reader it may seem that Corso is rebuking the Mexican zoo for not giving him something spectacular, sensational or exotic with which to conclude his poem. Here the presence of "ordinary / American cows" (*ll.* 26–27) does not permit the poet-narrator to sensationalize or fetishize the "foreign," but instead it initiates an encounter with his own cultural identity. Edward Halsey Foster states,

"Transcendence in Corso's poetry is found through language and surreal vision" (135), but such "transcendence," finally, is not achieved here in "Mexican Impressions." The surreality of the cow in the zoo, to Corso, confirms the superiority of a normalcy by which the poet reads the world; the absence of other animals, particularly ones indigenous to Mexico, in this poem is telling. The zoo is temporarily defined by the poet's amusement at the ridiculousness of America as an exoticized object.

Stephenson insists that the "theme and the element of delight are manifest in virtually every poem, every play and prose piece that Corso has written" (*Exiled Angel* 8). Corso's literary works are praised for their "zany humor, their vitality, and their immense energy — their enthusiasm, exuberance, and excitement" (Stephenson, "'The Arcadian Map'" 80). Yet the poem "Mexican Impressions" seems more invested in stasis. The "ordinary" cow, as strange or as ordinary as it may seem to Corso outside of American national boundaries, has been isolated from context as have been the other images in the five sequences: old Indian, boy in a sombrero, windmill, dead horses, and finally "ordinary" cows. They are material for the poet's own projected restlessness and alienation. If it can be interpreted that Corso acknowledges that all cultures exoticize or patronize each other, in ways that, ultimately, "zooify," then reciprocation is noticeably absent. In *Questions of Travel: Postmodern Discourses of Displacement*, Caren Kaplan reminds us that the "tourist is not ... free to move about willy-nilly in a libertarian world. If the tourist traverses boundaries, they are boundaries that the tourist participates in creating; that is, an economic and social order that requires 'margins' and 'centers' will also require representation of those structural distinctions" (58).

In terms of "structural distinctions," the United States, in this poem, seems oddly reconciled with itself; home is no longer the "messy, fragmented Babel of a place that America ... has usually been" (Elliott 247). These impressions are part of a flat, but fragmented, travelogue. What the poet-narrator learns from what he looks at in the Mexican zoo is that the details of a spectacle are relative. Corso may want "the image or observation that is astonishing in itself" (Foster 136), but at this exhibit he finds nothing extraordinary, except that as an American, no matter how much the outsider, he is on display, he is an Other. A case can be made that it makes him uncomfortable to be the object of a gaze, as if he were on display in a foreign zoo, but clearly it is disconnection from Mexico that Corso appears to seek most.

As an individual, Corso sees little or nothing that motivates him to want to connect with Mexican culture or people. "Gregory saw nothing romantic in the poverty and filth of Mexico City and wanted to leave as soon as possible" (Miles 216); similarly, "Tired of the poor living conditions in Mexico City and around Kerouac's apartment [at Orizaba Street which Kerouac shared with Burroughs's friend Bill Garver], Gregory Corso moved into a posh hotel" (Schumacher 243). These are the actions of a man not simply disaffiliating but actively disengaging from the culture around him; from the start of this poem sequence, at least, it is clear Corso may not go beyond merely looking at Mexico from physical and psychic distances.

As stated earlier, in the first two lines of the poem sequence Corso writes, "Through a moving window / I see a glimpse," which shows that this poet is more invested in separation than in linkages in "Mexican Impressions." The poet-narrator also remains in a moving automobile and glimpses what passes by. Ginsberg reminds us that "Corso's contribution to the whole [Beat movement writing] thing was that the line was a unit of thought.... And the reason it's a unit of thought is that's what you wrote down on that line" ("Improvised Poetics" 21). In the units of thoughts here, and throughout the sequence, Corso imposes judgments, reproofs Mexico, admonishes the country's social conditions and ultimately "enjoins explicit cognition," both in the last three lines of this poem and throughout the poem "Puma in Chapultepec Zoo." Corso chooses a solitary and centralized position which empowers him to dismiss everything he looks at but prefers not to "see," a rejection of his potentially powerful role as poet-*seer*.

The poet-narrator's sense of separation is certainly enjoined with the "motif of confinement" which provides the ultimate image in "Mexican Impressions" and "the central image for 'Puma in Chapultepec Zoo'" (*Angel* 23). In his introduction to *Gasoline*, Ginsberg writes: "Corso is a great word-slinger, first naked sign of a poet, a scientific master of mad mouthfuls of language. He wants a surface hilarious with ellipses, jumps of the strangest phrasing picked off the streets of his mind" (7); that characterization clearly does not apply to "Mexican Impressions," although Corso certainly begins "Puma in Chapultepec Zoo" with "mad mouthfuls" of words: "Long smooth slow swift soft cat" (*l.* 1). From this point on, however, the words become less aural, less lyrical and the intentions behind them less playful. These moments in the zoo, when he sees the puma pacing in its cage, seem to interrupt Corso's hilarious surface.

Corso significantly reduces the playing field, his canvas of Mexico, to the size of the puma's cage: "this 9x10 stage" (*l.* 5). "Puma in Chapultepec Zoo" is a poem that promises a spectacle, as if something of great value. Direct critique of the puma's confinement — certainly a synecdoche for a critique of most things Mexican — is basically sublimated to an organizational structure of questions directed at the puma:

> What score, whose choreography did you dance to
> > when they pulled the final curtain down?
> Can such ponderous grace remain
> > here, all alone, on this 9 × 10 stage?
> Will they give you another chance
> > perhaps to dance the Sierras?   [*ll.* 2–7]

Each of these questions contains a connotation of despair; the reader understands that the narrator's stance here is of observer of the downcast. "The poem begins with a description of the caged puma, emphasizing its grace and beauty, and contrasting the narrow closeness of the animal's present confinement with the expansiveness of its former freedom in the mountains" (Stephenson, *Exiled Angel* 23). Finally, Corso states it simply: "How sad you seem" (*l.* 8), which could as easily be said of Mexico as of the caged puma. Here is an example of empathy or at least sympathy that is seemingly absent in "Mexican Impressions," sadness as one route toward engagement. The word "seem," though, makes all this insight precarious, vulnerable or illusory.

The caged animal, in this poem, is centered in a theatrical setting created specifically for voyeurism. In this case, the heavier costs are being paid by the object being observed. By foregrounding this caged puma in a place where the natural is forced to exist in unnatural settings, Corso turns to image and language in order to make sense of a disturbing moment in an excursion into Mexico that was meant to be potentially filled with mad adventure. This brief poem calls the following observation into question: "Corso's poetic vision is itself a revivifying force, restoring language to innocence, celebrating wonder and mystery, remaking the world" (Stephenson, "'The Arcadian Map'" 81). It is the lack of innocence that informs this poem; the intention behind the existence of the "9×10 stage" (*l.* 5) may ironically destroy the cat's "ponderous grace" (*l.* 4). It is as if Corso, as poet, becomes responsible for recapturing these images of the world, but not in order to "restore" or "revivify" the world and articulate it through language and images. This puma does not keep Corso in Mexico, nor does he blame the country for any act of barbarism; immediately, the poet is returned to the life he has known in the United States.

"Puma in Chapultepec Zoo," like "Mexican Impressions," becomes a way for Corso to write himself back home, to that which is not alien and foreign, and to a place where he does not feel helpless and resigned. As a poet Corso can control the image of the caged, if not the forces behind the caging. Corso achieves this insight through a most circuitous path; namely, he realizes that the puma in the cage in Chapultepec Zoo reminds him of a friend back in New York:

> How sad you seem; looking at you
> > I think of Ulanova
> > locked in some small furnished room
> > in New York, on East 17th Street
> > in the Puerto Rican section.   [*ll.* 8–12]

Note that even as he records a profound connection between the confined puma in Mexico and a Puerto Rican friend who evidently finds New York less than habitable, Corso writes himself and his readers back to New York. In *Gregory Corso: Doubting Thomist,* Kirby Olson states:

> Corso writes often of zoos in poems ... because they accentuate the captivity of animals, but he always implies that the metaphor is easily reversible to show the captivity of the animal-like instincts in humans. Corso shows a special affinity for those creatures that lie somewhere between humans and animals ... because they help to erase the humanist line that reserves a special place for humanity [37–38].

In the space of this poem, the friend and the animal become one, both confined, outside of their "homes." Remember that this was a period when "the mid-fifties television portrayed a wonderfully antiseptic world of idealized homes in an idealized, unflawed America" (Halberstam 508). Corso doesn't attack the medium of television for the most part; Skau explains: "[h]aving grown up before the advent of television, Corso frequently focuses his attack on the print medium" (35). The key phrase in David Halberstam's quote is "antiseptic world," the notion that any cross-cultural or cross-class interactions might actually "infect" the discourses of hegemony. Ulanova, the Puerto Rican, is "locked" into his fate like the puma. Does Corso think of his own years behind bars and those spent in detention, or does he automatically and unthinkingly link a Puerto Rican friend with a puma because of their inherent parallel lives as primitives being on exhibit for civilization? Or is Kirby Olson correct that for Corso the zoo "metaphor is easily reversible to show the captivity of the animal-like instincts in humans" (38)? One thing is clear, the poem ends without Corso speaking for Ulanova; he respectfully notices the sadness in lives "locked" into their fates but does not turn them into his mouthpieces.

In rhetorical terms, Corso foregrounds the notion of dislocation but blatantly omits himself from questioning its center or textual margins. The poet-narrator stands outside of the implications, which are serious ones. Corso positions himself outside of his "motif of confinement" in a space that is free, although, admittedly, if he feels sadness for the friend and the puma, then Corso experiences a sad freedom. Interestingly, New York City appears to confine his friend but evidently it does not confine him. Corso, as observer, is outside of a need for "another chance" either in Mexico or in the United States. He is more invested in the poem than in the actual suffering that goes on long after the poem is written; Corso invests in the poem where "*Images* of violence, destruction, and death, of isolation and alienation are prevalent." (Stephenson, "'The Arcadian Map'" 80, italics mine).

Stephenson explicates one of the dominating themes of "Puma in Chapultepec Zoo":

> Despite the specificity of the poet's association, I think that by extension both the situation of the caged puma and of Ulanova ... may be read as metaphors of the human predicament: the spirit caged in the material world, vision locked in the senses, beauty and grace held prisoner in a fallen world [*Exiled Angel* 23].

The "spirit caged in the material world" may be applicable to the puma or to Ulanova in this "fallen world," but clearly Corso does not include himself in any such "caged" metaphor; he may be out of his element, so to speak, but he anticipates that he is *not* imprisoned in Mexico or his own outsidedness. Like the Mexicans in "Mexican Impressions," the fallen are the outsiders. Any vision of hope or transcendence is withheld by Corso, a vision locked in the poet's psyche. Once the puma and Ulanova are turned into convenient literary devices, their individual suffering or frustrations become peculiarly disconnected from their actual circumstances. Corso is willing to pay this price for the opportunity to discuss the state of being imprisoned, in general; it is important to note that when this state is "universalized," the markers of human and feral sufferings become someone else's currency.

Here not only does Corso withhold a vision of potential freedom, but he also prevents the reader from participating in any sense of Bakhtin's "openended present" ("Epic and Novel" 7). In this poem, Corso again does not provide a Bakhtinian "living contact with unfinished, still evolving contemporary reality" ("Epic and Novel" 7). This observation hinges upon line eight and the beginning of line nine in the poem, where Corso states: "How sad you seem; looking at you / I think of Ulanova." First, note the semantics of the puma "seeming" sad but without the narrator going so far as to judge the animal as being sad; Corso does not explicitly state that the puma is sad. Similarly, the poet-narrator states that he is "looking at" the puma, which is an interesting word choice to pick over "seeing," for example. "Looking" contains much more connotation of distance, objectivity and disengagement; also, what is looked at lacks agency. Again, the poetic impressions do not add up to a narrative but instead center the narrator, outside of the poem, as negotiator of the perceived world. Now, note the beginning of line nine: "I think of." What a long mental leap to think about a New York friend, Ulanova, who is dislocated in that city because of his Puerto Rican heritage. It is interesting how Corso comes to this realization here, now, in Mexico, and how it becomes so oddly connected to back home.

Inherent in this observation is the connection between an American friend in a New York City barrio and a dark, wild animal. In "Puma in Chapultepec Zoo," Corso reduces his friend to something feral, a thought process which reifies "the persistent Western tendency to process the third world as 'primitive'" (Torgovnick 13) and its masses as similarly "primitive." In Corso's poem, this comes dangerously close to racism, conflating a "person of color" into a wild animal of color. This odd juxtaposition causes a rather revealing gap in Corso's thought processes. Ulanova loses any "completedness as a whole as well as in each of [his] parts" to borrow Bakhtin's phrase regarding human orientation in time and in the world ("Epic and Novel" 30). In Stephenson's "Arcadian" article, he states: "In 'Puma in Chapultapec Zoo' the poet again depicts the unnatural confinement of that which is by nature free and self-sovereign. The caged puma epitomizes the general condition of sentient consciousness in the material world, as does the poet's friend in a faraway city 'locked in some small furnished room'" (79). If the puma and the Puerto Rican friend are "by nature free and self-sovereign" then the poet must be too. Perhaps Stephenson would suggest that Corso has reasons other than racist ones for making the connection, but then why displace himself? Here, in this poem, Corso does not attempt to stand on the margins with puma or friend; he seems to gaze at the two from the center, an observer who sees but cannot imagine himself in the scene, for he remains aloof.

This poem's sense of displacement suggests that the animal and the friend may be "free" and "self-sovereign," but they are confined by outside forces, which evidently the poet-narrator does not feel here in this poem. The poet-narrator's sense of separation from the United

States, then, is all that may be enjoined with the "motif of confinement" providing the ultimate images in "Mexican Impressions" and "Puma in Chapultepec Zoo." As poet-narrator, Corso chooses to stand outside of cultural, hegemonic locations and instead observes these discrete cultural sites from a position of privilege. In Mexico, Corso finds "foreign" sites, and those sites he might also find in New York City if he were a disempowered outsider, which clearly he feels he is not in these two poems, at least not as their author.

Corso is disaffiliated from any active stance to Mexico's realities throughout these works; it is clear that he actively wishes to disengage himself from the culture around him. As stated earlier, his gaze is unidirectional. In "Mexican Impressions," the poet-narrator remains inside his car, looking at Mexico pass, from the highway; he is disassociated from the political implications of either poverty or capitalism. At the end, Corso may be out of the car but now he is at a zoo, which creates a similar structural division in terms of the touristic gaze. That same gaze chiefly informs the second poem, but with differing implications.

These two Corso poems about Mexico reveal a writing strategy in which the poet constructs veils or walls to keep himself at a safe distance from those about him. Only inside the space of these poems does Corso find Mexico manageable, a country generous with its "grim landscape ... expresses[ing] the graceless, hopeless, merciless character of the physical world. In such a world the poet (and the spirit) is a prisoner, an exile and a victim" (Stephenson, "'The Arcadian Map'" 80). This world allows for Corso to employ "images of light, radiance, illumination, warmth, and color, and of classical and medieval grandeur to suggest the ineffable splendors of the world of the spirit" ("'The Arcadian Map'" 80). It is important to understand that Corso "arrives" in Mexico but immediately begins writing himself back home. He is anxious to return home, where his real interests and struggles lie. Poetry's potential power of transformation has little to do with the "the doomed Mexican child, the windmill 'alone, alien, helpless' in a windless, cactus landscape" ("'The Arcadian Map'" 80). In these works, Corso wants internal transformation rather than transformation through external experience.

The Corso poems looked at here are engaged in notions of dislocation and home. Corso's strategy to deal with his reactions to being "away" and dislocated is to center hegemonic "Americanness." Indeed, the idea of "going foreign"—so central to Jack Kerouac and Allen Ginsberg, for example—does not appeal to Corso, at least not as far as Mexico is concerned; no "constant state of spiritual questing" (Lardas 168). Furthermore, any poetic vision of hope or transcendence is not to be found in these two poems; those living in Mexico, in Corso's vision, are strangely lacking in any apparent or obvious acts of free will. Here there is an implied fatalism by which nothing can be restored because Mexico is, indeed, a country with a "stricken landscape" which is peopled by easily summed-up individuals who function as preconceived images for the writer-tourist. This dismissal emphasizes Corso's poetic vision of Mexico as one with a closed present, in which implications of history, culture and everyday realities may be considered, but their totalities, their complexities, are ultimately irrelevant.

Mexicans are present in "Mexican Impressions," but they neither speak nor act. They are presented as lacking agency, doomed by the country they were born into, just as the puma was doomed to be captured in the Sierra Madres in "Puma in Chapultepec Zoo." Its confinement in a Mexican zoo "embodies all that is cruel, blind, limited, and retrograde—a heavy, dreamless, 'petrific bondage'" (Stephenson, "'The Arcadian Map'" 79). Corso finds Mexico and things Mexican to be quite native, indeed primitive; inherent in that situation is a sense of irredeemable despair. Corso is not interested in the Bakhtinian notion of interaction: "In [the] actively polyglot world, completely new relationships are established between language and its object (that is, the real world)" ("Epic and Novel" 12). Corso's "real world" is dismissed beyond its affability as image or literary source.

As poet-narrator in these two works, Corso chooses to stand, generally, outside of the Beat stance of opposition to American hegemonic locations. Clearly he prefers the position of American privilege, specifically as he observes and catalogs Mexico's abjection. These poems then become vehicles for this poet to write himself back home, to that which is not foreign and alien and to a place where he does not feel helpless and resigned. What is achieved in these poems, particularly in section five of "Mexican Impressions," is that Corso recognizes that what is most "ordinary" is the Americanness from which he feels he cannot escape, or from which he chooses not to escape (conditions which are not the same). Halberstam's observation of the Beats, where he claims that they "revered those who were different, those who lived outside the system" (300), becomes ironic when applied to these two Corso poems. Corso's intent, in these works, seems to end up becoming an attempt to center home and location, over that of travel and adventure.

More important than his apparent inability to escape from the culture's bifurcated system of conformity or opposition is Corso's underlying desire to be at the center of its dominant discourses, partly because this position provides him with an identity that insulates him, however falsely, from the rest of the world. Corso's sense of displacement in Mexico reinforces his sense of separation from the United States, which ultimately provides a nostalgic wish to be back home; consequently, he writes himself *back* home through "Mexican Impressions" and "Puma in Chapultepec Zoo."

4

Allen Ginsberg

Allen Ginsberg's "Siesta in Xbalba AND Return to the States," as the compound title implies, are two poems melded into one. Indeed, the "poem is built around the contrast indicated by the title" (Moramarco 222). Section two of the poem, clearly, is the "Return," but Mexico and Ginsberg's Mexican experiences linger throughout the work, so I treat it generally as one work, although I divide it up here into two sections and multiple "parts" for clearer discussion.

Ginsberg's major trip to Mexico leads him to the ancient Mayan ruins of rural Chiapas which is evidence of his courageous spirit, keeping in mind that the "[tourist] gaze must be directed to certain objects or features which are extraordinary, which distinguish that site/sight of the gaze from others" (Urry 92). Ginsberg's journey also emphasizes his intellectual curiosity, a hunger for a past that is *new* to him. As Kaplan points out, historically, "powerful masculinist discourses, adventure and exploration writing proved to be instrumental in the construction of rationales for imperialism" (53). It is in the spirit of "adventure and exploration writing" that in 1952 Allen Ginsberg embarks, via Cuba, on his exploration of the Maya country; he camps out at several ancient sites and meets up with friend Karena Shields at Palenque. He begins to write a long poem, "Siesta in Xbalba AND Return to the States" (its compound title will be explicated later), at her *finca* near the border of Guatemala, which becomes a work of adventure and exploration. The first part of the poem—Ginsberg's "Siesta in Xbalba"—foregrounds experience at its most heightened level, a goal for most of Ginsberg's literary output. He offers an unabashed queer view from his unique perspective, but it is one that interestingly departs from "powerful masculinist discourses," perhaps because of his own hybridized perspective(s) and his "metonymic relationship with America" (Lardas 90).

In his book *Allen Ginsberg,* Thomas F. Merrill succinctly characterizes Ginsberg as a "Jewish, homosexual, raised in a household strangely presided over by a politically obsessed mother on the ragged fringes of sanity and an utterly straight conventional father (himself a poet and high school teacher), Ginsberg inevitably felt himself the lonely outsider" (8–9). This "lonely, Jewish, homosexual outsider" will, eventually, expand his poetry to return the role of the poet to the center of a literary and historical universe through confrontation with the mainstream which is inevitable because the "homosexual's sense of persecution is not a fantasy, but a social reality, and yet he is made to feel his anxiety as his own distortion" (Bergman 34). Ginsberg comes to reject this distortion of his self in the world, choosing instead to recreate a psyche that is not simply without distortion, but enlarged to a dramatic scale which allows contradiction and, indeed, confrontation to be expressed aloud and loudly.

David Bergman, in *Gaiety Transfigured: Gay Self-Representation in American Literature,* attempts to enlarge what he, among others, finds unique in the gay, literary voice: egolessness, or "a narcissism without a reflection" (45). Bergman generalizes that "gay poets are far less present in their work" (47), a prescribed masking becomes both the rhetorical strategy as well as the subject. Ginsberg, then, deploys a complex writing strategy within Bergman's analysis — someone who is not present, but who creates a new persona bearing his own name and who is omnipresent, a persona that foregrounds the struggles or the pressures to be silent and remain less than visible. Doty writes: "Not only is he exiled from the tranquilized suburbs by virtue of ethnicity, sexuality, political philosophy, and intellectual energy; he also cannot locate in the codified possibilities of American society a tenable way of living" (143). The codified options as poet and citizen do, indeed, prove untenable for Ginsberg, although he himself must make peace with his many identities and his vision of joining his body and his mind.

On a personal level, Ginsberg's literary voice reflects some notions of egolessness in the guise of self-questioning and self-doubting; on another level, Ginsberg expands his consciousness into the realm of a cosmic self, which is all ego, all narcissism *with* a reflection. The exploration of the interior self can often require a Whitmanesque accounting of the exterior world. This exterior world, in the wilds of Chiapas, however, manages to be inclusive of Mexico and things Mexican but not Mexican people (since it is such a remote region). This unpopulated foreign space, then, helps Ginsberg avoid ideological spaces and problems that his Beat compatriots, Gregory Corso and Jack Kerouac, do not avoid in their 1950s poems about their own travels in Mexico. It frees Ginsberg to work on finding a voice that becomes inclusive of the history of the *homo sapien* without necessarily denying the particularities and centrality of his own experiential realities and hunger for poetry. There is a danger to this course of action, of course, for revelation of the cosmos inevitably changes the daily. Bakhtin confirms that "The world becomes polyglot, once and for all and irreversibly. The period of national languages, coexisting but closed and deaf to each other, comes to an end. Languages throw light on each other: one language can, after all, see itself only in light of another language" ("Epic and Novel" 12). This insight can be extended beyond just language, but also the perception of the world and of human purpose under the sun.

Ginsberg's new poetic persona encompasses an emerging "hyperbolic sense of self" (Bersani 95), an exaggerated self. A self that is all ego becomes Ginsberg's mature persona, a self that is global — perhaps even greater and grander than global — manifests itself in the poem "Siesta at Xbalba." But again, even here there are egoless qualities to it, as his voice takes on an ennobling tone; self-interest and becoming-interested-in-self prove to be distinct acts. Personally, Ginsberg seeks to position himself outside of the machinery of capitalism and patriarchal imperialism; his primary challenge, not distinct from all such "Beat" challenges, is to transcend hegemony. The "Beats viewed their contemporary America as disconnected from its natural source, creating a neurotic atmosphere of fear and repression" (Lardas 133). Indeed, Ginsberg's program is one of nonparticipation in the U.S. war machine and its attendant structures of social and cultural support. "The fault for the condition of Ginsberg's generation — and his own violated psychic state — thus lies with 'Moloch,' the embodiment of the State as evil, the demon of this world" (Doty 143). Ginsberg, then, situates his literary role as a great and grand cosmic being who has been forced to exist because of capitalism's aggressive destruction of all gods other than its own. In adopting the role of the poet — a cultural speaker who has been labeled both a prophet and a madman — his role is powerfully transformative for himself and his readers.

The elements of Ginsberg's self-questioning and self-doubting can likely be traced, primarily, to both the anti-Semitism and the homophobia rampant in America in the decades of the 1940s and the 1950s (and obviously beyond). Critical disregard — if not out-and-out critical loathing — for the literary period or genre of poetry categorized as "confessionalism" was, and is, partly a hegemonic reaction to the mapping of the margins, the disenfranchised in American society: women, gays, people of color and the working class. Reconsideration of the confessionalist project is a means by which to include not only new questions but new answers.

While ego-centered, Ginsberg is not trapped within the static constructions of his own life. In the provocative book *Homos*, Leo Bersani reminds us that "Confession is a form of ventriloquism" (12) — which is particularly apropos of Ginsberg's form of confessionalism. His poetic works cannot be reduced to one individual's confessions; instead, they are the works of a cosmic self inscribing himself/itself into the discourse of the center, a form of "ventriloquism." There is the ventriloquist and his or her "dummy," the perfect illusion of the constructed nature of dichotomies. Ginsberg's strategy is the following: "the field of action is a triangle of *dharma*, the superego, and the poet. The problem is to break down dualisms, and in this sense, narcissism is a step on the way" (Burns 271). Confessionalism, it is assumed, derives from the ego, but Ginsberg's project begins to supercede such an assumption by positioning himself in the mythic space of the cosmic ego rather than the individual one.

Not one to stay hidden for long, Ginsberg emerges in poetry with "a hyperbolic sense of self and the self's renunciation of its claims on the world" (Bersani 95). This quote from *Homos*, in a chapter entitled "The Gay Daddy," seems to be at the heart of Ginsberg's intent in this poem. Ginsberg positions himself, like Walt Whitman, as a prophet of the cosmos, which becomes evident in the poem "Siesta in Xbalba":

> I alone know the great crystal door
> > to the House of Night,
> a legend of centuries
> > — I and a few Indians.
>
> And had I mules and money I could find
> > the Cave of Amber
> and the Cave of Gold
> > rumored of the cliffs of Tumbala. [*ll.* 238–45]

Here Ginsberg may assume a position that is like a "tourist [who] straddles eras" (Kaplan 62), but that position is not merely topographical, an insight which helps him transcend a tendency to imperialize location or place. His life, his poetry and the interstices between the two form a map of the universe outside of "an increase of territory, an imperialization" (Kaplan 89). His sense of election ("I alone know....") requires Ginsberg to discover, to explore, to offer his heirs treasures that he alone can distribute through his poetry.

Keeping in mind, as Kaplan reminds us, that "movement of deterritorialization colonizes, appropriates, even raids other spaces" (89), Ginsberg projects himself beyond the topographical; his cosmic self, his narcissism *with* a reflection, expands his consciousness into the realm of history, which is a temporal and spatial universe. The poem rests upon very vivid details, a poem built "out of simple notations" (Foster 110); yet, the space traversed here is more cosmic than geographic, which allows Ginsberg a wider range of space than may exist outside of borders and territory. This moment in Ginsberg's growth as a poet, and as an openly gay man with a public identity, is summed up in the following way: "He washed away ten years of New York soot in a tropical paradise" (Miles 160). Geography and the metaphysical self are juxtaposed in Ginsberg's time in Mexico; here the forces shaping his voice as a sort of translator of the cosmos is being nurtured, rehearsed and tested.

Ginsberg's "Siesta in Xbalba AND Return to the States" begins with reflections of being in Palenque, but by the twenty-eighth line of the work Ginsberg is ruminating about the years in New York and the circle of friends and acquaintances left behind. In fact in *As Ever*, the poet remarks about his Mexico jaunt: "This is a rare & marvelous trip I need to feed (& free) my soul from 10 years of New York City" (159). In a journal entry dated April 16, 1954, Ginsberg writes:

> No god to look for, but the old legends and better the old buildings before they're ruined by time.
> I left that party in NY for peace—to sit out at nite in front of the thatchroof shelter on a bench sounds of an alien tongue, crude Mexican and a moment when the plenilunar cloudfilled sky is still and small [*Journals* 52].

Mexico, then, offers Ginsberg an experience to grow, as an individual and as a poet. "The Beats' well-known penchant for traveling ... not only symbolized their constant state of spiritual questing but functioned (albeit loosely) as rituals of perception by which they gained a new perspective on the values of the dominant culture" (Lardas 168–69). Poetic maturity or growth for Ginsberg means placing himself outside of his clique, outside of New York City, and into a situation which is out of the ordinary for him, namely the alien and crude. His "need to feed (& free)" (*As Ever* 159) his soul suggests a conscious attempt to go beyond prescribed ideological borders. New York City, as a demarcated center of U.S. capitalism, can be characterized as an opiate which hinders a Bakhtinian moment of interillumination for Ginsberg's early works; it was not "the zone of maximal contact with the present (with contemporary reality) in all its openendedness" ("Epic and Novel" 11). After Mexico, Ginsberg is determined to deploy an "openendedness" in his urbanity.

In regard to the title of this Ginsberg poem, it needs to be stated that the region of Chiapas on the Yucatán peninsula, where he stayed, the Karivis [or Karvis] Indians call Xibalba "(pronounced Chivalva), and the Mayans believed it to be a region of limbo or purgatory" (Miles 160); however, "[when] writing the poem ... Ginsberg misspelled the proper name. He elected to leave the misspelling intact in the published work" (Schumacher 162). This may be interpreted in a number of ways. Ginsberg may simply be ignoring notions of historical or cultural authenticity or defiantly refusing to respect the native spelling out of a sense of superiority; one or both of these notions may have informed his choice. The space that Ginsberg chooses to travel here is as much psychic as it appears to be topographical; thus, the Xbalba in his mind does not have to conform, necessarily, to the Xibalba of mythical geography. So Ginsberg's "Xibalba" reflects the internalized map of an externalized quest, "the scene of the vast and eternal" (Schumacher 278). The misspelling, then, is a faithful account of misperception which is itself one of the major themes of this poem.

The "siesta," as the poem opens, is clearly an artistic moment for this poet since it is presented, forthrightly, as the initiation of a literary moment: "Late sun opening the book, / blank page like light, / invisible words unscrawled" (*ll.* 1–3). Beginning with a siesta seems appropriate: "Tourism necessarily involves daydreaming and anticipation of new or different experiences from those normally encountered in everyday life" (Urry 14). Several lines later, Ginsberg displays his self-satisfaction with this place and a potential wish to stay "perhaps a lifetime":

> —One could pass valuable months
> and years perhaps a lifetime
> doing nothing but lying in a hammock
> reading prose with the white doves
>   copulating underneath
> and monkeys barking in the interior
>   of the mountain
> and I have succumbed to this
>   temptation —   [*ll.* 9–17]

Initially it seems that, as Fred Moramarco characterizes it in his article "Moloch's Poet," "[lying] in a hammock in a small Mexican village, Ginsberg toys with the idea of staying forever" (222). His daydreaming or "idea of staying forever" is somewhat undermined by a Ginsbergian sense of paranoia that quickly creeps in and undermines the sedentary, optimistic sense of calm which this poet initially experiences. Ginsberg writes:

> eyes watching me:
> unease not of the jungle
>   the poor dear,
> can tire one —
>   all that mud
> and all those bugs...
>   ugh....   [*ll.* 21–27]

Here, any "idea of staying forever" seems temporary, particularly in light of this unease, which appears in lines twenty-one and twenty-two of this 504-line poem. What those "eyes" are is not clear; in this portion of the poem there are only animals, insects and "things," so whether Ginsberg imagines that animals from the jungle, or perhaps unseen natives, are watching him in the hammock cannot be assessed. The "ugh" reinforces the idea that this Mexico is not a literal paradise but a psychic one, rewriting the land and people inhabiting Ginsberg's thoughts.

It is at this point in the poem that Ginsberg dreamily recalls his time in New York as "an eternal kodachrome" (*l.* 29). Moramarco characterizes this moment of the poem: "The narrator's attention shifts back and forth from the hammock to the party in New York, and the experience of straddling the two worlds in his imagination allows him to objectify both of them by stepping outside of himself and observing his participation in both" (223). This moment of objectification does not seem to possess a neutrality or a dispassionate tone, for the "eternal kodachrome" suggests a nostalgia for what is lost and may be irretrievable — except through meditation or poetry.

The memory of New York begins in the twenty-eighth line — "Dreaming back I saw" — and concludes at the sixty-second line. Here the poem shifts back to Palenque, but more importantly the poem returns to alternating its poetic lines between unindented and indented lines; throughout the New York "section," Ginsberg keeps his lines flush left, orderly and perhaps comformist. The poem's form itself mirrors Ginsberg's struggle against restrictive order and dangerous chaos; the strategy of mapping out his own process of association requires him to write in a free verse that is not entirely free of literary traditions.

To reiterate Moramarco's last point, Ginsberg relates "the experience of straddling the two worlds in his imagination" (223), but it is more than two worlds in which Ginsberg traverses here. Besides New York (and America), there is Xibalba, the "real" place, and also the other place: Xbalba, the place he inhabits subjectively. Interestingly, Moramarco continues, Ginsberg opens a path of introspection and evaluation "by stepping outside of himself and observing his participation in both [worlds]" (223). This is nowhere more obvious than in the last several lines of the New York section; those lines critique, frankly, his New York circle. Ginsberg in "Siesta in Xbalba" states of his friends and acquaintances posed in that "eternal kodachrome":

> all posturing in one frame,
> superficially gay
> or tragic as may be,
> illumined with the fatal
> character and intelligent
> actions of their lives.   [*ll*. 57–62]

Perhaps for the first time in a profound way, Ginsberg objectifies his own position outside of New York's art circles and his own spheres of influence or ego. Clearly he reifies his own daring adventure to Chiapas, Mexico, as something that builds up from the "superficially gay or tragic," which cannot be underrated in terms of both adventure and self-growth. He chooses not "to posture" within the New York lifestyle, but ironically he does adopt the posture of cosmic poet and of the adventurer whose own "character and intelligent actions" are not fatal. He has escaped the conformist confines of the first world, at least physically.

After line 62, after the conclusion of the New York remembrance, Ginsberg returns to the present. Rather than lying in his hammock, he finds himself

> in a concrete room
> above the abandoned
> labyrinth of Palenque
> measuring my fate,
> wandering solitary in the wild   [*ll.* 63–67]

It is at this point that it becomes clear that Ginsberg's poetic persona is enlarging into a self grander than one usually ascribed to a single individual. To become a prophet, a shaman, Ginsberg must inflate his individuality to cosmic size. Place proves useful to the possibility of a trance-like state that melts away the actual world in favor of the perception of the possible (and some might say "probable") world.

In the poem, Ginsberg "[leans] against a tree" (*l.* 76), but comes to see "himself / leaning against a tree" (*ll.* 83–84), a most omniscient position. Then, briefly in the poem, Ginsberg fails to elaborate on what he may see from this new hyperbolic position and simply shifts to a brief flashback — back to New York again. He is bound to the city and his friends in ways that he must articulate:

New York, and Ginsberg's years in Harlem, represent:

> …the noise of a great party
>   in the apartments of New York,
> half-created paintings on the walls, fame,
>   cocksucking and tears,
> money and arguments of great affairs,
>   the culture of my generation…   [*ll.* 85-90]

Interestingly, the use of the word "cocksucking" seems so Ginsbergian to the contemporary reader, but it is rather outside of the tone of this particular poem. In his book *Great Poets Howl: A Study of Allen Ginsberg's Poetry, 1943-1955*, Glen Burns characterizes this moment in the poem:

> This is the last mention of the party back there, located somewhere in time and space. About this passage it can be noted that it is one of the first confessional moments in Ginsberg's poetry in the process of coming out of the closet. It is also one in a series of attempts to 'remember' his generation, to record the despairs, ecstasies, and hopelessness.... This will be the last mention of the New York he has left behind; from this point on the poem stays where it is or moves toward the future [271].

Before Ginsberg can stay where he is or "move toward the future," he has to center not himself but this new poetic grand self, a sort of prophet of the cosmos. "The half-created paintings on the wall" are emblematic of his own complex identity; the writing of this poem contributes significantly to Ginsberg's gay identity, one that is distinctive among all of the Beat writers. A key phrase in this quoted passage is "my generation," for Ginsberg does not separate himself from his peers nor admit to his own marginalization in their groups' sexual experimentation(s), which for Ginsberg solidifies his orientation. This is a distinct difference. Importantly, he has come to imagine his own sexual orientation, with its ecstasies and tragedies as central to his generation and not merely individual lifestyle or desire choices.

Having accomplished this, Ginsberg is poised to put New York behind him and immerse himself in the here and now, Mexico as subject. Throughout lines 63 to 129 there is an emphasis on the "I" which arguably characterizes Ginsberg's mature poetic *oeuvre*; in "Siesta in Xbalba" the pronoun appears thirty-two times (which shouldn't surprise any serious Ginsberg reader). In the context of this poem, the first-person pronoun, as well as "me" and "my," reify Ginsberg's new place at the center of the universe as a sort of prophet or shaman. The early stages of the poem's illumination begin after Ginsberg momentarily returns to his paranoiac state, where he has an

> —uncanny feeling the white cat
> sleeping on the table
> will open its eyes in a moment
> and be looking at me— [*ll.* 96–99]

The sense of "eyes" watching him again evokes suspicion or paranoia, and it appears two more times before section one concludes. It is as if the jungles are filled with mirrors. Ginsberg eventually realizes that he has been projecting himself into the world, and that illusion is one major cause of paranoia and pain. Stepping back, developing a cosmic self and then reentering the world becomes his strategy for survival. In line 72, he admits that "my soul might shatter" which reinforces the notion that this is a dangerous journey before "the scene of the vast and eternal" (Schumacher 278).

Ginsberg then turns his attention to what is around him in Chiapas, to

> recording the apparitions in the field
> visible from a hammock
> looking out across the shadow of the pasture
> in all the semblance of Eternity [*ll.* 101–04]

At this point in "Siesta in Xbalba" before Ginsberg tackles this notion of "Eternity," the poet-narrator begins a cataloging of what he sees from his reclined position. Again, rather than people, we get things: a roof, a slope, vegetation, a mountain, trees, a ridge, the sky, the air, clouds, palms, rain, fronds, the wind, the ground and, interestingly, "monstrous animals" (*l.* 122). Perhaps these are the animals first watching Ginsberg from the thick vegetation. Then as we read the lines which lead up to line 129, we get a sense that night is upon us and that triggers in Ginsberg "a moment of premonition" (*l.* 127). Here again, akin to the mention of "Eternity," Ginsberg pulls back from abstraction and returns to the specific.

Obviously Ginsberg teases his readers by withholding cosmic notions which we know as faithful readers that he will investigate, in time; it helps to build a bit of tension on the reader's part, and structurally it seems meditative, as if he is focusing on specifics to arrive at the abstract after lengthy thought. More importantly, before we can arrive at any "illuminative seizure," we, as readers, have to go through the night with Ginsberg, which neatly ties in with Xibalba. Indeed:

> According to Mayan mythology, Xibalba was a region of purgatory or limbo.... To Ginsberg, who had come to Mexico with his creative imagination still suspended between the mysticism of his Blake visions and the objective realities of his *Empty Mirror* poetics, the purgatory image was apt, compelling. He had ventured to what appeared to be one of the early points of civilized time, yet he was still only a good plane ride from the most modern manifestations of civilization. Having witnessed both, he was, in his own mind at least, suspended between them. Xibalba and the Mayan ruins of Mexico were places of contemplation [Schumacher 162].

In short, we may not arrive at illumination until we pass through limbo or purgatory with Ginsberg, as if we were also reenacting some ancient Mayan ritual. The self in this poem is linked to the hope of a collective identity for humankind; Ginsberg's personal experiences are to be paths by which the reader may travel.

Merrill appropriately sums up the poem to this point:

> Friends are trivial but 'I' am serious is the note Ginsberg seems to strike; but the usual comic trump card remains to be played: the oncoming mystic vision.... There is an inchoate quest operating in the debris of mind that has fallen down, and it seems to be directed toward the eternity that is so often the misty goal in Ginsberg's poems.... If eternity is the 'bond of time'—the element that glues everything together into community and permits everyone to be an angel—then it is reasonable that an access to this state [including drug use] is well worth the price [103].

Merrill reiterates that there is an "oncoming mystic vision" (103), but rather than Ginsberg directly addressing it early in the poem, he simply alludes to visions through abstractions, using the terms "eternity" and "premonitions." Ginsberg continues to sort through the "debris of mind that has fallen down" (Merrill 103) in his cataloging of things

Mexican before arriving at "the misty goal," to use Merrill's term (103). The poem is on the verge of some kind of interior event, one that suggests that the unfolding moment and the eternal moment are linked with the past.

Ginsberg seems to be always writing *for* home (at least his return in the near future); he provides an alternate sense of history and culture to the United States, as well as to the world. This is a part of "the inchoate quest operating in the debris of mind that has fallen down, and it seems to be directed toward the eternity that is so often the misty goal in Ginsberg's poems" (Merrill 103). In "Siesta," Ginsberg is engaged in a journey toward Mayan history and culture, but only as a means to reinvigorate the present rather than simply reiterate the past. By combining autobiography and myth in order to enlarge his awareness and literary voice to cosmic levels, Ginsberg moves from the level of vivid details, detached observations, local color and exoticism into a transcendent tapestry of history as an essential component to present realities. To achieve this, Ginsberg sometimes utilizes the effects of drugs to aid in this quest. Lines 130–132 read: "So spent a night / with drug and hammock / at Chichén Itzá on the Castle." Barry Miles, in *Ginsberg: A Biography,* clarifies this point of the poem and the drug Ginsberg took to achieve his illuminative seizure: "On his first night there, high on paracodin, he climbed the ninety-one steps to the top of the great pyramid, hung his hammock in front of the main entrance to the summit chamber, and lay for an hour in the tropical night. Bats flew around the ruin, and the forest seemed to close in on him" (157). The "inchoate quest," however, is not toward the Mayans but, seemingly, toward his own imperfect and dubiously formulated relationship ("metonymic relationship" [Lardas 90]) with the United States.

To arrive anywhere, it seems that, we, as readers, first must pass through the metaphorical purgatory that "Siesta in Xbalba" invokes along with the poet-narrator: "a region of limbo" (Miles 160). There are numerous word choices, most of which are repeated several times, reinforcing this sense: "dark," "night" and variations of the word "night," "ruin(s)" and "soul(s)," to name the more obvious ones. The poem begins with a "Late sun" (*l.* 1), which has shifted to darkness and night by this point in the poem. Here Ginsberg states:

4. Allen Ginsberg

> I can see the moon
> moving over the edge of the night forest
> and follow its destination
> through the clear dimensions of the sky
> from end to end of the dark
> circular horizon.   [*ll.* 133–38]

Among the stones there are large openings, "portals" (*l.* 139), through which he views "illegible scripture, / bas-reliefs of unknown perceptions" (*ll.* 140–41). As his lamp flickers, the poet narrator sees "a deathshead / half a thousand years old" (*ll.* 147–48), which becomes one of the central images of the poem.

At this point in the long poem, the death's head begins to function as a metaphysical portal to another time, but a portal very much in the same location. Indeed, the death's head embodies the "fine thought" (*l.* 162) of the artisan who made this stone sculpture, and those thoughts across the centuries now connect with Ginsberg's thoughts in the present here in the poem. Ginsberg as poet-artisan becomes connected to the unknown artisan who sculpted this figure. "He sat before a death's-head and wondered about the unknown artisan who carved it" (Miles 157), just as the reader of this poem wonders about its poet-narrator who takes us on this distant journey. Merrill explicates the significance of this moment in "Siesta in Xbalba"; he states:

> Time and eternity, as the glue that binds everything together, is developed as a concept later in the poem when Ginsberg meditates upon a 'death's-head.' Part of his fascination lies in its relevance to the principle of prophecy.... Here is an instance of eternity indeed obliterating time but in the fashion of biblical prophecy. The anterior artisan, the maker of the head, sculpted his artifact until it fully represented his idea; but now, Ginsberg muses, the death's-head communicates that idea across time [104].

The journey into Mayan history and culture, here, becomes an interrogation of the meaning of art across time, which reinvigorates Ginsberg's role as cosmic poet in the present of this poem. Notably the emphasis is on what this object of art and its creator say about Ginsberg the creator. We are returned to the core of Ginsberg's persona as prophet: "'Siesta' became a statement of the general cultural situation of his time" (Burns 239). Mexico and New York City are merely sites of arrival and departures, unlike all the other potentialities in a prophet's all-embracing vision.

Importantly, as readers, we now seem to be arriving at Ginsberg's objective in this poem: a transcendence of not only historic time but also of geographic space. Keep in mind that the full title of this combined poem is "Siesta in Xbalba AND Return to the States." Thus, central to this work is spatial transcendence as well. Note also how the "AND" insists on the relationship between locations through the power of the poet. Here, midway through the first section of the poem, "Siesta," Ginsberg finds himself situated "on a time-rude pyramid rebuilt / in the bleak flat night of Yucatán / where I come with my own mad mind to study / alien hieroglyphs of Eternity" (ll. 173–76). Juxtaposed against the Mayan artisan is Ginsberg himself; and, juxtaposed against these "alien hieroglyphs of Eternity" (l. 176) is this poem itself, as it is being written and as it is being read.

The "inchoate quest," finally, is an imperative for this Beat poet to assume a cosmic role; however, in typical Ginsberg fashion, he keeps a sense of grounding through self-doubt, bawdy banter or a sense of humor that is impeccably human and ordinary. As the poet-narrator stands here on this ancient pyramid, intently studying hieroglyphs with his "own mad mind" (l. 175), suddenly something startles him: "A creak in the rooms scared me. / Some sort of bird, vampire or swallow" (ll. 177–78). The inclusion of a possible "vampire" makes the humor here focused and earthy, if not mythic. From this point on, we get several lines of a cataloging of the auditory sense of the place, from "metallic / whirr of chicharras" (ll. 182–83) to "weird birdsong / or reptile croak" (ll. 189–90).

As the poet narrator begins to fear that his wavering candle "will go out" (ll. 195–96), Ginsberg evokes "the names of the pre-Columbian civilizations which flourished in this place, Ginsberg surveys the surviving ruins and notices how they have become intertwined with the natural landscape. Nature's work, and man's, has become one with the passage of time" (Moramarco 226), just as Ginsberg's quest to the Yucatán becomes one with the nature of his identity, as a person and as a poet. Similarly, time and space are transcended:

> Time's slow wall overtopping
>   all that firmament of mind,
> as if a shining waterfall of leaves and rain
> were built down solid from the endless sky
>   through which no thought can pass. [*ll.* 219–23]

Here the poem returns to a sense of endlessness, or eternity, but it is one through which Ginsberg's thoughts, or anyone's, apparently cannot pass. This appears to be in contrast to the poet-narrator's sense of transcendence from temporal and spatial limitations. Here, then, time appears to have limits; indeed, it has a "slow wall" (*l.* 219), which may be more about mortality as the end of personal time than the end of any universal time.

In *Dharma Lion: A Critical Biography of Allen Ginsberg,* Michael Schumacher states that "Ginsberg wanted his poem to have the qualities of a siesta, that peaceful limbo between an awakened consciousness and death—a consciousness which ... had a visionary quality of its own" (169). When Ginsberg states in line 229 that he "— was looking back / with eyes shut...," the reader is supposed to assume this is Ginsberg "looking back" with "eyes shut," which is a visionary stance, "a limbo between an awakened consciousness and death" (Schumacher 169). This supports Moramarco's conclusion that "Siesta in Xbalba," is "a meditation on time, death, and eternity as day turns to night in the poem" (224). Also central to "Siesta in Xbalba" is Ginsberg's emerging persona which now contains a hyperbolic sense of self: a self that is global—perhaps even greater and grander than global. There is "a yearning for apocalyptic vision" (Merrill 102) which is realized only through the rejection of the poet as removed observer. Ginsberg is in the process of discovering how to use the details of his life as the bases of cosmologies (even if sometimes contradictory), a process that culminates in a revolution within poetry: "The Beats crashed through the restraining mask of the removed artist — the Flaubertian tradition that saw the artist as God, omnipresent but invisible.... The objective camera eye of 'The Waste Land' would be replaced by the 'I' of the personal 'Howl'" (Tytell 16). Ginsberg's challenge is to take eternity and make it subjective without denying narratives greater than the individual self.

This strategy of identity formation is specifically informed by Ginsberg's homosexuality. Bergman hypothesizes:

> The homosexual child experiences a sense of limitlessness, an otherness unbounded by the forms and shapes of his parents. But being free of any specific form, the child is free to put on any numbers of masks ... in some Whitmanesque expansion, absorb within himself the various styles around him [36].

Ginsberg is aware that his role as a poet follows the path traveled by Whitman, who "invites us to view him as the supreme egoist, a kosmos through which the afflatus is surging and around which no orbit can be swept by a carpenter's compass" (Bergman 48). Gay American poetry has no other major literary predecessor who formalizes sexual orientation as an important center of perception, which makes Ginsberg's kinship to Whitman primary. This connection, this choice of strategy, extends from the Platonic to a very contemporary model of gay sexuality:

> Through sex, the nonreproductive sex of the homosexual, the homoerotic act moves retrograde — not to future generations, but back to former generations. The gay man or woman, unburdened of the forms of heterosexual love so easily degraded into property considerations, achieves a kind of communion with the dead and becomes the vehicle through which they speak and make themselves manifest [Bergman 207].

Ginsberg's poetic "act moves retrograde," and he finds himself aligned with Whitman in a tradition of "communion" not only "with the dead" but with the godhead as archetypal father. "But his realization of a connection with the past also makes him aware of a specific tradition to which he — as a contemporary American poet — is related, as well as a future to which he has an obligation" (Moramarco 227), and this informs "Siesta in Xbalba" which centers death but pushes out toward a sense of the future in which all things may be made manifest.

This sense of the future emerging from metaphoric death rather than a sense of a linear past is key to queer identity. Gay men, raised outside of their biological tribe by heterosexuals, generally, become their own parents in the sense that they must raise themselves, at least partly, outside the norms of the mainstream definition of family. "As a homosexual, Ginsberg was in a position to know very well how oppressive a society could be if one did not conform to accepted patterns of behavior" (Foster 85). Oppression ends up losing some of its power through an actively queer sense of identity, despite its myriad individual and collective costs. Ginsberg becomes his own father, emotionally and symbolically, as well as his own son. Ginsberg writes in "Notes Written on Finally Recording 'Howl'": "The universe is a new flower. America will be discovered. Who wants a war against roses will have it. Fate tells big lies, and the gay Creator dances on his own body in Eternity" (83). To extend the metaphor of self-parenting (or "self-creating") along Christian lines, gay men embody both God and the Christ-child, which is surely an inflated, even hyperbolic, sense of self.

Integral to that hyperbolic sense of self — the emergence of the Whitmanesque shaman-prophet — is a passage contained in this section of the poem, which also happens to be one of the most interesting portions of "Siesta in Xbalba" as a whole. Ginsberg writes:

> I alone know the great crystal door
>
> to the House of Night,
>
> a legend of centuries
>
> — I and a few Indians   [*ll.* 238–41]

That this is a passage of exaggerated or hyper-inflated self-confidence seems evident, perhaps made stronger by the poem's following four lines:

> And had I mules and money I could find
> the Cave of Amber
> and the Cave of Gold
> rumored of the cliffs of Tumbala   [*ll.* 242–45]

Ginsberg is at no loss for ego here, but first let's return to lines 238–41 for they are important here.

These lines are significant to the poem here for they are one of the only places in the poem which contain actual "Mexicans," in this case "a few Indians" (*l.* 241). Perhaps the first thing the reader will notice is that Ginsberg positions himself as "I alone..." (*l.* 238), even as he qualifies it three lines later as " — I and a few Indians" (*l.* 241). This blatantly dismisses the "natives" to a subservient role in this "discovery"; they have neither agency nor voice, but become part of the scenery of this discovery being lead by the poet-narrator. This strophe begins "I alone know..." (*l.* 238); the next strophe begins "And had I mules and money I could find" (*l.* 242); finally, the strophe after that one begins "I found the face of one / of the Nine Guardians of the Night" (*ll.* 246–47). Clearly, Ginsberg is centered here, and the Indians are relegated to superficial individuals fulfilling unimportant roles, observers of their own history.

The self-confidence with which Ginsberg states that he discovered "the great crystal door / to the House of Night" (*ll.* 238–39) has possibly hoodwinked at least one critic. In *Great Poets Howl*, Burns states: "Ginsberg actually did find 'the great crystal door...', a cave on Mount Aavalna whose presence existed only in legend" (286); I take Burns's word choice of "find" to mean "discover," particularly in light of the fact that he states its "presence existed only in legend." In fact, "a few Indians," as Ginsberg states in "Siesta," knew about its existence and took Ginsberg to it after an earthquake in the area in which the poet was traveling. Miles summarizes Ginsberg's experience "finding" the legendary cave:

> The next morning, he rose early and went to the gate to look at the view of the Hunacmec valley.... The Indians wanted him to come with them to the east side of the mountain, where there was a

4. Allen Ginsberg

huge cave. Two of the men had been there many years before, and they wanted to know if the earthquake had destroyed it.... When Allen reached the head of the column, he found all the men lined up on stones and rocks in front of a drop. Above them towered the huge arched entrance to an immense cavern.... House of Night — dark cave [162].

The cave was still there, and Ginsberg reported it to the proper authorities. "In response to the information provided by Allen, a team arrived from the *Instituto Geologica* with generators and equipment to measure the cave, which turned out to be one of the largest in the Western Hemisphere" (Miles 163). Ginsberg may have played a role in making its existence official, but he did not discover it as such, for the local population not only knew about its existence but its exact location.

From this point in the poem, Ginsberg makes a shift from specific topography to a global range of places. From "these ruins" (*l.* 255), Ginsberg begins to wax nostalgic for "the classic stations / of the earth" (*ll.* 257–58): New York, Europe, Arabia. As if Ginsberg "could go / no further before heaven" (*ll.* 267–68), he turns his attention here to his next travels, in the immediate future. He asks, "Toward what city / will I travel?" (*ll.* 319–20). This speculation returns him to his reflections of his last decade in New York, where he sits

> seeing in dreadful ecstasy
> the motionless buildings
> of New York rotting
> under the tides of Heaven   [*ll.* 332–35]

The questioning and reflecting on the past brings the poet-narrator out of the present: the moment among the Mexican ruins. Burns characterizes this moment in "Siesta in Xbalba":

> The series of rhetorical questions belongs to an oratorical form that will break forth in a few months in 'Howl.' The siesta is over. Ginsberg is on his way back to the *samsara* world, and at this moment — just when his poem lifts itself out of the meditative atmos-

phere of death — heads and ruins, time and eternity, the writer and writing, the appearance and erasure of signification — he recalls his vision in Harlem in 1948.... And now, out of his long meditation, he breaks into prophecy. The verse form is the same as the memory snap-shot at the beginning [288].

Ginsberg's journey has conflated his person, and here he makes the most significant move toward "Howl," which personifies this poet's mature career as prophet-critic of America and its Moloch-like qualities. Ginsberg arrives in a very "new" world, one which parallels Bakhtin's version of events in Europe: "its emergence from a socially isolated and culturally deaf semipatriarchal society, and its entrance into international and interlingual contacts and relationships" ("Epic and Novel" 11). These "interlingual contacts and relationships" contain the potential to make contact across isolation and to complicate the patriarchal systems in place.

At this point in "Siesta in Xbalba" as a result of his intense spiritual and physical journey, Ginsberg realizes:

> There is a god
> dying in America
> already created
> in the imagination of men
> made palpable
> for adoration:
> there is an inner
> anterior image
> of divinity
> beckoning me out
> to pilgrimage.   [*ll.* 336–46]

The poet-narrator has made a significant, indeed a key, connection to the United States as a result of his journey. The poem, then, becomes about Ginsberg, the person and the poet, and about America in the

1950s, rather than about Mexico or Mexicans. The poem shifts from Mayan history and an adventurous quest motif to self-realization. If Burns is correct that "Ginsberg himself was fully aware that if death was the center of 'Siesta,' he was nonetheless moving away from that point" (283), then the question becomes what does he move toward?

What he may be moving toward is contained in the last line of this section of "Siesta," where Ginsberg states: "O future, unimaginable God" (*l.* 347). To arrive at that future and unimaginable being, he must first topple the false, or evil, powers. One of these powers is the one he will continually joust with: the United States as a capital-driven superpower; thus, Ginsberg's journey in "Siesta in Xbalba" maps the emergence of his life's journey, from his "self-shattering" of conformist identity due to his outsider status as a Jew and a homosexual to the shattering of false gods. Naturally, Ginsberg does not shatter the United States and its sheer, brute power, but he does attempt to shatter the illusion(s) of it, a proper step after recognizing and pointing out its hegemony.

Keeping in mind, as Bersani states, that "self-shattering is intrinsic to the homo-ness in homosexuality. Homo-ness is an anti-identitarian identity" (101), Ginsberg's new role as shaman-prophet emerges out of a new recognition of the power of his complex identity, which from "Siesta in Xbalba" onward is a politicized, empowered and global identity.

Moramarco says that the "second section of the poem is more easily summarized than the first" (229). In many ways the second section is a look at the "disconnected manuscript" which requires a linking between the writer of text and the reader of that same text. "There is a 'Jump in time' to the future when Ginsberg begins his return to the States, carrying with him some lingering images of his Mexican experience" (229). Among these "lingering images" is an apocryphal image "in white mist" (*l.* 364):

>   ...a heavenly file
> of female saints
>   stepping upward
> on miniature arches
>   of a gold stairway
> into the starry sky,
>   the thousands of little
> saintesses in blue hoods
>   looking out at me
> and beckoning:
>   SALVATION!   [*ll.* 370–80]

That this "beckoning" image appears as Ginsberg looks "toward the stations / of the classic world" (*ll.* 361–62) reinforces the sense that out of his quest in Mexico the goal is to return "home," to the United States, no matter how ambivalent his relationship to it may be. Indeed the poem's shift to "home," characterized as "abrupt" by Burns (289) may reinforce his anxiousness to return after the poem's "meditative, accumulative circularity" (Burns 289). Ginsberg returns a changed man with a new power to change those around him.

Section two of "Siesta," from this point forward, will be referred to as "Return to the States." At this point the overall poem is clearly marked with the Roman numeral for two. Also, Ginsberg makes a very prosaic statement to mark the poem's shift; he writes:

> Jump in time
>   to the immediate future,
> another poem:
>   return to the old land
> penniless and with
>   a disconnected manuscript,
> the recollection of a few
>   sensations, beginning: [*ll.* 348–55]

This realization is immediately followed not by these "recollections" but by details and brief narratives concerning Ginsberg's journey back to the United States.

Separation from "location can never be assuaged by anything but return" (Kaplan 33); in actuality, however, there is more than that which drives this poet toward the United States. On some level, Ginsberg is satisfied to be leaving Mexico behind him; in *As Ever,* Ginsberg writes: "My Spanish is got to a point where I can find out what I want easily but I keep making mistakes that have cost me money from time to time" (164), and elsewhere, "I am beginning to really hate mexico & almost wish I were out of it" (165). In *Dharma Lion,* Schumacher states that "Ginsberg's Mexico trip ... began to wear on him.... His financial and physical woes made him short-tempered with the locals, with whom he was having trouble communicating" (161). Journeying back to the States, the poet makes a major stop to see the mummies of Guanajuato. "In the second half of the poem, 'Return to the States,' the focus of the reverie shifts from Mayan ruins to mummies at Guanajuato, which suggest what true immortality is" (Foster 97). Regarding the mummies, Burns tells us, "Ginsberg is able to read the dance of life, frozen as it were in 'timeless reflex,' as eternal as the party photo" (292).

Here, again, this poet first assumes a comic, human role before he centers himself in his more cosmic role as shaman-prophet, interjecting into this scene in the poem — the viewing of the Guanajuato mummies — that sense of humor so ordinary and wonderfully human. As the poet-narrator stands looking at the mummies "in soiled / funeral clothes" (*ll.* 399–400), he humorously characterizes them as "knock-kneed, / like burning / screaming lawyers" (*ll.* 401–03). If it is true, as James Breslin states, that Ginsberg "is a mystical and messianic poet with intense suicidal wishes and persistent self-doubts ... whose most spontaneous thoughts characteristically turn toward feelings of being stifled and inhibited, walled and bounded in" (403), then here in the presence of these effigies of physical death certainly Ginsberg's "longings for some painful, apocalyptic deliverance — ultimately death itself" (Breslin 403) is subordinate to his will toward the future, to go on living. Indeed, Ginsberg's

> Whitmanian style is founded upon the celebration of the secular world as an inexhaustible resource of sensation and identity. The world of Ginsberg, on the other hand, is the world of the ruined mind presiding over the death of its physical being and attempting to refound itself in a new reality. The culture of Ginsberg's poems, despite its attempt to naturalize itself, is fundamentally an international or extraneous phenomenon [Grossman 106].

Finally, at this point in "Return to the States," Ginsberg confronts the abstract notions of "death," "eternity" and "self" as the comic tone gives way to serious considerations. The poet-narrator reflects momentarily and concludes:

> The problem is isolation
> — there in the grave
> or here in oblivion of light.
>
> Of eternity we have
> a numbered score of years
> and fewer tender moments
> — one moment of tenderness
> and a year of intelligence
> and nerves: one moment of pure
> bodily tenderness — [*ll.* 429–35]

That we have a limited time upon this earth is the lesson the poet-narrator takes from the visit to the hallways of mummies in Guanajuato. Suddenly, here, the poem reads: "I could dismiss Allen with grim / pleasure" (*ll.* 436–37). This is certainly one moment where multi-voicing becomes foregrounded in this poem; this statement clearly suggests that there is an "Allen" distinct from the poet-narrator.

Are there two Allens? Many Allens? Who is speaking here? One obvious reading of these lines is that the poet-narrator speaks from the shaman-prophet position; this other "Allen" is the man, small and human. It is the small and human (and male) Allen that here makes a mental note to himself about a sexy, voyeuristic recollection he had spying on a two men and two women in an adjoining hotel room in San Miguel: "The male look through a kind of 'porno-tropics' is endless voyeuristic" (Urry 151). In typical Ginsbergian fashion, the sexual play leads to utter joy and holiness:

> What joy! The nakedness!
>   They dance! They talk
> and simper before the door,
>   they lean on a leg,
> hand on a hip, and posture,
>   nudity in their hearts,
> they clap a hand to head
>   and whirl and enter,
> pushing each other,
>   happily, happily,
> to a moment of love...   [*ll.* 446–56].

This human "moment of love" is one Ginsberg watches but is not a part of; here he is part voyeur and part omniscient god-figure. Also, it prefigures a dominant theme in Ginsberg's works; indeed:

> Nakedness; physical, emotional, psychological, was to become a recurrent theme of Ginsberg's poetry. This openness to life and experience is characteristic of the Beat project, and would in itself be enough to mark it as an oppositional tendency in the late 1940s and 1950s without the spirit of protest and revolt picked up on by most critics when *Howl and Other Poems* appeared in 1956 [Docherty 200].

Out of the scene with the two couples engaged in sensual play, the poet realizes: "What solitude I've / finally inherited" (*ll.* 457–58), a moment of existential awareness. While it is true that "Ginsberg's figure of desire, in the geographical space that informs his work, is folded on the human body, another geography, with topological precision" (Burns 238), he inevitably returns to his own body and loneliness.

Typically, in Ginsberg's textual landscape, physicality (and sexuality) is prioritized. In *As Ever* (dated February 18, 1954), Ginsberg writes: "Well I am still here in the state of Chiapas & don't know for sure when I will leave, maybe next week maybe next month. Doesn't depend on anything for sure, just when I come out of a sort of retreat or limbo & push on for bright lights alcohol & sex joys" (186). This succinctly reinforces Ginsberg's wish to retreat from New York, to find himself (again). Ginsberg's position here in the poem as voyeur leads him to an existential moment rather than a sexual one, which clearly supports Bersani's observation that "sexual behavior is never only a question of sex, that it is embedded in all the other, nonsexual ways in which we are socially and culturally positioned" (3). Ginsberg emerges from an oppressed position in general society, and here in Mexico he finds transcendence in a cosmic persona. He is a shaman-prophet, but it is clearly an earthy role if he is spying on sex play. It is an omniscient stance, as if he has his eye to the keyhole to Eden, watching two Adams and two Eves discovering each other.

Ginsberg then returns to the present on his fifteen-hour bus ride toward Mexicali, a town on the California border. These last images of Mexico clearly reify some of Ginsberg's negative feelings toward Mexico. That the last image of Mexico in "Siesta in Xbalba AND Return to the States" is "of the 'garbage cliffs of Bordertown' in Mexicali, the *barrios* of a lost colonial empire" (Burns 286) is not heartening. Inscribed here is a nostalgia for empire he doesn't critique, at least at this point of his career. The bus ride, similarly, was unpleasant: "... fitful, / gazing, sleeping / through the desert" (*ll.* 468–70), but more importantly Ginsberg presents us with a racialized image of his neighbor on the bus: "beside a wetback / sad-faced old-man- / youth, exhausted" (*ll.* 471–73). Is it because he is heading toward the United States that Ginsberg reverts to this offensive remark about a "wetback"? Also telling is that Ginsberg sits next to this "old-man-youth" and finds nothing sexy about him; typically, Ginsberg finds anyone sexy, but certainly males. This moment reveals a Ginsberg without a libido, as if the "wetback" does not warrant his lust, his fantasies.

Arriving at the border, Ginsberg declares it "the end of a trip" (*l.* 484); the scene is described clearly:

4. Allen Ginsberg

>   ...garbage cliffs
> of bordertown overhanging
>   the tin house poor
> man's village below,
>   a last night's
> timewracked brooding
>   and farewell,
>   the end of a trip.   [*ll.* 477–84]

From the transcendence among Mayan ruins to the present is a remarkable passage marked by descent into "reality." The journey, the quest, into the jungles of Chiapas seem to have come to little that is positive physically; yet, the trip into deep Mexico was not about a physical journey so much as a spiritual quest to find his literary persona. It could be true that Ginsberg, here, is noticing the unfortunate realities of the border between the U.S. and Mexico, a place where U.S. influence is particularly heightened. Indeed, the penultimate strophe reveals this quest to have been immensely successful on another level:

>   — Returning
>   armed with New Testament,
>   critic of horse and mule,
>   tanned and bearded
>   satisfying Whitman, concerned
>   with a few Traditions,
>   metrical, mystical, manly
>   ...and certain characteristic flaws   [*ll.* 485–92]

Ginsberg conjoins his own identity, particularly his homosexuality, with the profoundly prophetic tradition, much in the manner of Whitman. Ginsberg's future poems, from this point forward, will be like new testaments. As this poem's final strophe makes clear, one of those testaments will be devoted to his adversary: U.S. hegemony. Indeed, as this poem concludes, the reader can hear the Ginsbergian chant of America as a new Moloch about to emerge:

> The nation over the border
> grinds its arms and dreams
>   of war: I see
> the fiery blue clash
>   of metal wheels
> clanking in the industries
>   of night, and
> detonation of infernal bombs   [*ll*. 494–501]

At this point, exhausted from his trip, Ginsberg conflates the United States into the size of one generic city, where "the silent downtown / of the States / [sits] in watery dusk submersion" (*ll*. 502–04). Ginsberg's new hyperbolic sense of self, his new literary persona, contains the power and the authority with which to confront the United States and the powers that be over the long career he has in front of him.

"Siesta in Xbalba" offers us a view of a poet who is redefining himself on a very grand scale. "There is a new tone of self-confidence from the trip which has canceled the decade of defeat in New York" (Burns 295). "Siesta," then, is a poem partly about the Mexican culture, particularly in regard to its Mayan heritage, but "Siesta in Xbalba" focuses upon Ginsberg's resentment of being forced into a narrow existence between cultures within his own United States. As a Jew and as a homosexual, Ginsberg as poet speaks about "Americanness" in a new way, which parallels his personal journey through the experiences of a (temporarily) self-exiled individual. That he leaves New York, siestas in Chiapas, and now is about to relocate to the San Francisco area reinforces the sense that this trip to Mexico brought about a profound psychic passage for Ginsberg (and for us, as readers).

Brian Docherty reminds us, in his chapter "Allen Ginsberg" in the book *American Poetry: The Modernist Ideal,* that: "There were, of course, other poets in the 1950s writing as gay men, notably Robert

Duncan and Frank O'Hara, but Ginsberg is the pioneer closet dismantler. Whitman, however, is the American trailblazer" (Docherty 201). Ginsberg's reclamation of Whitman's stance as gay and prophetic is counterhegemonic to America in the 1950s, which makes "Siesta in Xbalba" new in terms of modernism. In terms of a gay-and-proud identity in modern poetry, "Siesta in Xbalba" becomes a sort of benchmark, at least in the sense that Ginsberg will come to personify homosexual pride more directly and powerfully than any U.S. poet before him. It is important to understand that Ginsberg leaves the safety of culturally constructed "gay" sites such as bars, theaters, homes of friends. He travels the United States and Mexico, assuming that the right to view landscapes and mindscapes is his. Opting for the world about him instead of its artificial constructions through agreed-upon gay sites, Ginsberg extends the geographical possibilities of gay lives.

This is not to say there aren't profound issues regarding gay identity in Ginsberg's *oeuvre*. There is Ginsberg's reluctance to fully come to terms with the ambivalent sexual natures of Kerouac and, specifically, Neal Cassady, as well as his blatant disregard for the importance of women and female sexualities.

> No wonder Joyce Johnson called her book *Minor Characters*, an accurate reflection of the importance of women in the lives of the Beat writers, and of the part women were allowed to play in the counter-culture revolution. If that revolution was a failure, it was because any revolution which incorporated the oppression of women into its structure (as well as alienating the working classes) could not succeed. Nevertheless there were significant gains, and Ginsberg and the Beat writers achieved a great deal in terms of sexual liberation and personal liberation, and helped to bring about a change of consciousness which cannot be reversed [Docherty 215].

In regard to women, it must be noted that Ginsberg's friend (and host) Karena Shields is as absent from "Siesta in Xbalba" as is contemporary Mexico; "women, if mentioned at all [by the Beats], function primarily as the background for white male activity and evolution" (Lardas 178). Shields's absence reveals a great deal, particularly considering that Ginsberg's actual "Return to the States" was with a monetary loan from Shields and that his "Siesta in Xbalba" would not have been fully possible without the extension of Shields's hospitality to this counter-culture poet, who was invited to stay at her ranch in Palenque.

Aside from those thorny issues, Ginsberg's trip into deep Mexico becomes, ultimately, a quest to find a literary persona to suit his emerging poetic voice. Ginsberg begins to acknowledge his role as spokesperson for the disenfranchised of the Beat movement; thus, he comes to view his cultural role as a spokesperson *for* home, a shaman-prophet large and powerful enough to challenge the hegemony of the 1950s United States. Ginsberg's "Siesta in Xbalba" characterizes the emergence of the Ginsbergian self and expands his poetic *oeuvre* into the territory of testimonials. A self that is pure ego becomes Ginsberg's mature persona: a poet's role as global and cosmic in character manifests itself in this poem. Ginsberg's chief challenge is to transcend U.S. hegemony, but here, in "Siesta," that task can only be a start. First, Ginsberg must claim his oppositional ground before he can begin to move beyond it and situate himself outside of the dialectical role of counter-culture guru.

As Ginsberg's role traverses across both space and time to connect with this cosmic self, his brand of confessional poetry addresses the smaller self, Ginsberg the person, rather than Ginsberg the prophet. That this poet plays both roles in his poetry reinforces the polyvocal nature of his intent. There may be confession here in "Siesta," but at the same time there is "ventriloquism," to return to Bersani's concept, for poems like this one — and there will be many more to come from Ginsberg — are partly spoken in the voice of a provocatively cosmic self. By combining autobiography and myth, enlarging his awareness and literary voice to cosmic levels, Ginsberg moves into a transcendent tapestry of time, space and history. This tactic allows the hyperbolic sense of self its necessary space.

5

Denise Levertov

Denise Levertov is more than a distant observer of Mexico, its culture and its history, partly because Levertov moved there to *live* in the country with her American husband, "a fluctuating palimpsest in her living journey" (Rodgers 23). Unlike most of the poets who were born in the United States and visited Mexico in the 1950s to write about it (William Carlos Williams, Jack Kerouac, Gregory Corso, Allen Ginsberg and Robert Hayden), Levertov's time in Mexico cannot be characterized as merely a visit; she made it her home, even if temporarily so; Levertov tells Pacernick: "I have never really 'belonged' anywhere, and therefore in some degree am at home anywhere" (92). Consequently, Levertov *is* writing *at* home, whether she is in New York or Guadalajara because her new home outside of Great Britain becomes where she is present.

Levertov's poems about Mexico in the 1950s, then, transcend the oppositional dialectic of location/dislocation, perhaps because of her position as a female poet-narrator; "the astute reader never forgets that Levertov sees from a woman's perspective, and what her poetry reveals is the complex nature of perception" (Hanson 75). Levertov's experiences, as articulated in her poems about Mexico, accentuate acceptance and welcome of the new, the different, rather than fearing or dismissing the foreign which often reveals cultural shortsightedness. In an interview, she states, "I'm glad to have a foot in more than one culture" (*NYQ* 9). In short, this "foot in more than one culture" helps her poetic vision to *see* beyond merely superficial *looking*. "Sight is viewed as the noblest of the senses, the most discriminating and reliable of the sensuous mediators between humans and their physical environment" (Urry 146), which is central to Levertov's works from the very beginning.

Levertov's poetry collection, *With Eyes at the Back of Our Heads*, was published in 1960 but certainly composed prior to that, so here I assume the works date from the late 1950s, approximately. In any case, Levertov continues to write about Mexico, in significant ways, into the 1960s and beyond. Although I end my brief study here with two poems from this collection, my work could have been further informed by "Five Poems from Mexico" in *The Jacob's Ladder* (1961) and beyond (which may well include material written in the 1950s). Certainly January, 1, 1960, did not usher in the beginning of the era of the counterculture and ethnopoetics; indeed, the 50s were significant to the decade to follow, for many of the seeds planted then (and some in the 40s, as well) found fruition over a period of time. For "Levertov, the poem makes not a complete record, not even a confirmation of hopes, but an honest critique of the self's progress as it tries, incompletely, to return to an ever changing image" (Jackson 209). This is evidence of Levertov's dynamic nature of intellectual inquiry.

Levertov's poems about Mexico frequently do not mention "Mexico" or a real Mexican place specifically, but allude to the Mexican landscape or at the least a tropical landscape. "Tomatlan (Variations)," "Overland to the Islands," "A Supermarket in Guadalajara," "Scenes from the Life of the Peppertrees," "Triple Feature" and "Xochipilli" are glimpses of Levertov's experiences in Mexico, which generally seem to move inward and upward. Levertov emerges as a philosophical and life-affirming observer of Mexico and its culture; according to Harris Frenkel, "Levertov portrays particular images that are not outside the ken of human experience, but that require an open receptivity" (24). It is this "open receptivity" and her own fluid position between and among cultures that allows Levertov to engage in dialogues with the "foreign"; she states, "I'm 'out of sync' because I have never related to European, or specifically English, literary tradition with that poignant concern and discomfort, that sting of self-consciousness" ("Williams and Eliot" 60).

Although Levertov, generally, does not advance polyvocality explicitly in her works, the poet engages the reader in the experience of Mexico. Her works demand that we, as readers, develop a Bakhtinian sense of "the listener as a partner-interlocutor" (Bakhtin, "The Problem" 66). This necessarily requires a rejection of the monovocal as each listener must now "translate," on many levels, what is being heard (or seen). Partnership also signifies a willingness to encounter others on their own terms and vice versa, although these interchanges may bring with them a new world, or even new worlds. "Movement is change, and change can be painful, but with admirable consistency the poet [Levertov] welcomes and celebrates change, despite its attendant inconvenience or pain" (Gitzen 128). The dynamism in her poetry confirms a poet's commitment to question her own position(s) in various discourses; further, she decenters herself from the hegemonic position of speaking on behalf of other human beings and even another country altogether. This characteristic may be one source of the curious criticism that Levertov is a distant, even "cool" poet as may be summarized by Juhasz's observation that this poet "is characteristically an observer, participating through sympathy or even empathy in the world around her but not through direct involvement; frequently, she as poet acts through the actions of others" (62). Levertov rejects the seduction of the monovocal even as she explores other possible strategies; thus, Levertov cannot be accused of inaction without being terribly misread.

Levertov forges new ways of looking and seeing experience; she does not merely relate local color, but attempts to immerse herself in the culture in very new ways. Significantly, Mexico becomes an opportunity for experience, rather than something feared, foreign or fantastically exotic. As a poet in multiple cultural spheres — Britain, the United States and Mexico — it seems fitting that she may be *at* home no matter where she is. In Bakhtinian terms, Levertov expands what may — or perhaps, must — be considered important in the writing and reading of a poem. Bakhtin expounds that

> Any expansion of the literary language that results from drawing on various extraliterary strata of the national language inevitably entails some degree of penetration into all genres of written language (literary, scientific, commentarial, conversational, and so forth) to a

greater or lesser degree, and entails new generic devices for the construction of the speech whole, its finalization, the accommodation of the listener or partner, and so forth. This leads to a more or less fundamental restructuring and renewal of speech genres ["The Problem" 65–6].

"Penetration," as used in this quote, is an overtly patriarchal term, but it does suggest the necessity of intentional disruption or movement toward the pleasure of language and the politics of meaning; it is not an accidental gesture. It may indeed be welcomed, as in a mutual sexual exchange in "Tomatlan (Variations)," or not — particularly if it means a reification of patriarchal order or systems. The Bakhtinian notion of "extraliterary strata of the national language" ("The Problem" 65) keeps at its center the literary, a naturalized geopolitical center which Levertov consistently rejects through most of her works.

Instead, Levertov consciously prefers being "intently haphazard" ("Overland" *ll.* 1–2); this is a strategy that requires precise language for the spontaneous experience of being alive; like her later poems, Denise Levertov's poems here "are strategies to assimilate, appropriate, and integrate a variety of experiences — of gender, nature, and spirit — to which she sought to remain open" (Hanson 75). Openness to experience can lead to a variety of experiences that may be described as "extraliterary"; Bakhtin's argument that the "extraliterary strata of the national language" leads to a "fundamental restructuring and renewal of speech genres" ("The Problem" 66) is intriguing because it suggests that multi-voicing is inherently a dynamic force, one that is not a respecter of dominant languages, ideologies or power systems. As Levertov investigates the actual, she finds the means to travel to the conceptual, as posited by Linda Wagner-Martin in her article "Levertov: Poetry and the Spiritual": "No matter what the world of humankind experiences, the drive of the artist — both natural and intellectual — is to reach for the positive, the light beyond the earthiness of the human" (199). Levertov does not seek to be "beyond earthiness"; she works hard to stay on the concrete and observable Earth. This is not so much a contradiction, but a possibility "to investigate man freely and familiarly, to turn him inside out, expose the disparity between his surface and his center, between his potential and his reality. A dynamic authenticity was introduced into the image of man, dynamics of inconsistency and tension between various factors of this image" (Bakhtin, "Epic and Novel" 35). These actions, for Bakhtin, arise from laughter, a potent weapon. Within Levertov's *oeuvre*, the willingness for discovery achieves similarly revolutionary ends.

Often in her works, the specificity of Mexico and its landscape and culture is relegated to the universal, which can be liberating, for it takes the Mexican experience outside of hybridity and places it within the context of the general; "what her poetry reveals is the complex nature of perception" (Hanson 75). This returns Mexico to the everyday, the ordinary, but in a more complex context than we have seen in the works of the other poets so far in this study. Mexico becomes more authentic as a country, not a country of mere foreigners. Levertov is *at home* because she chooses to exist in the places and times of her life even as she often transcends the specificity implied in any geographical location. "According to Levertov, the poet is part of the general existence and has to be in correspondence with her time and place" (Christensen 98). Levertov concludes "Overland to the Islands" with the line "not direction — 'every step an arrival.'" Levertov is at home even as she continues discovering the world.

The first poem in Levertov's book *Here and Now* (1957) that mentions Mexico is set in New York City. "Central Park, Winter, after Sunset" is about Central Park in the winter, obviously, but on a more general level Levertov widens the textual playing field of this literary work. The poem becomes as much about Indonesia or Europe (in the winter) as about New York's Central Park. Lights in the New York windows become "bells in Java" (*l.* 12), which convey a sense of "festival / but / somewhere far-off" (*ll.* 14–16); they are "sounds from / over water" (*ll.* 17–18). In the poem's final strophe, Levertov takes the "frosty field" (*l.* 19) and declares that its presence flows

> ... from
> Holland to Mexico:
>   space, or
>   space as dreams
>   dissolve it   [*ll.* 20–24]

It seems to me that this early poem is atypical of what a seasoned reader expects from Levertov, which is usually a poem based on real experience rather than dreamscape. Although this poem mentions Mexico specifically, it cannot be called a poem about Mexico. Instead, it interrogates the idea of space itself, space attached with names of nations and discourses of nationalism, a movement toward the realization that "[l]ocation is, then, discontinuous, multiply constituted, and traversed by diverse social formations" (Kaplan 182). Borders that dissolve necessarily introduce complex questions of location and dislocation. Questions posed from restrictive or monovocal language are typically hampered questions, questions that may not seriously interrogate the material at hand.

In "Central Park, Winter, after Sunset" Mexico — like Holland, Java and, arguably, New York — is an abstract concept, even though the names of these places are concretely present in the poem. Many of Levertov's poems arguably about Mexico frequently do not mention "Mexico" or a real Mexican place specifically, but allude to the Mexican landscape or at the least a tropical landscape ("The Palm Tree," "Pure Products," "Broken Glass," "Sunday Afternoon," "The Whirlwind," "The Lagoon" and "Pleasures," among others); although there is not space here to investigate the full range, including all these works might *reinforce* my major arguments but not necessarily *strengthen* them. The works presented here are poems about Mexico that may be representative of all of Levertov's poems about Mexico and works central to this particular investigation of poetic sightedness in Mexico in the mid-century. Although "Scenes from the Life of the Peppertrees" could fit into the category of poems I exclude as easily as the category of those I include, I discuss it here because critically it is one of Levertov's earlier "major works," according to some critics, and it has been reprinted frequently.

Here I focus on "Tomatlan (Variations)" from *Here and Now*; "Overland to the Islands," "A Supermarket in Guadalajara, Mexico" and "Scenes from the Life of the Peppertrees" from *Overland to the Islands* (1958); and, "Triple Feature" and "Xochipilli" from *With Eyes at the Back of Our Heads* (1960). In these works — whether Mexico is alluded to or mentioned directly — there are specific glimpses of Levertov's experiences in Mexico which open up issues of literary representation. In *Understanding Denise Levertov,* Harry Marten reminds us that Levertov "claims for her subject the mysterious workings of the imagination on experience" (12). Through a close look at these representative poems, I investigate the "mysterious workings of the imagination in experience" where Mexico is more or less explicitly her primary canvas.

In regard to the poem "Tomatlan (Variations)," Tomatlan, in the state of Jalisco, is on the Pacific coast; this detail almost needs not to be stated, as Levertov's short poem sequence here so clearly foregrounds a place by the sea. Virginia M. Kouidis, in her article "Denise Levertov: Her Illustrious Ancestry," characterizes the poem's title, "Tomatlan (Variations)," as recalling Stevens's "love of exotic place names" (258). Here Kouidis may be revealing her own exoticizing stance toward Mexico, rather than Levertov's. As someone who lived in Mexico from time to time, as someone who lived only slightly over 100 miles inland from Tomatlan, Levertov may have not found the place name "Tomatlan" exotic at all.

"Tomatlan (Variations)" is a sequence of four sections; it is a poem of sensuality that leads to outright sexuality. At the poem's beginning the sea is "quiet, shadow-colored and / without shadows" ($l.$ 1–2); here the sea makes no sound and is of a uniformly blackish, or intensely dark, color. From this still, dark scene emerges "the sea wind" ($l.$ 4), a transcendent thing. Instantly and swiftly, the sea wind moves "towards the / steep jungles" ($ll.$ 5–6), and ultimately becomes "the awakener" of the jungles and, perhaps, of the poet and her readers. It is this mimesis that initiates the poem's movement. From the "quiet sea" ($l.$ 1)— or perhaps read "passive" sea — comes an aggressor, an initiating force. Note also that the movement is from the Pacific coast to the inland, and up the "steep jungles" ($l.$ 6), which inverts the more predictable movement in a typical sea poem of moving outward, toward a watery horizon. Levertov here moves inward and upward, which seems fitting for this life-affirming poet. Her writing strategy reveals "a good poet devoted to developing concrete moments in which the numinous emerges out of the quotidian" (Altieri 226). This sense of emergence is central to finding energy and vision in the poet's surroundings instead of the poet's own imagination as the center of the site of observation.

In section two, the sequence's second variation, the sea wind takes the form of a "panther" (*l.* 9); the wind becomes personified and moves of its own accord, no longer a thing *of* the sea. The panther/wind continues the inward and upward movement toward "mountain jungles" (*l.* 11). In that process, the narrator feels the panther/wind against her body. The panther's (the wind's) "silky fur / brushes me" (*ll.* 12–13), she states; from the transcendent sea wind to the animal form, Levertov moves her variations toward a sensual experience, which becomes directly sexual in the next section. The panther is the sea wind, and the sea wind is the panther. Sensuality is one means of mapping the experience of Levertov's Mexico.

In section three, the panther is not evident; in fact, the sea wind has become something else. The "green palmettos of the / blue jungle" become women, shaking "their / green breasts, their stiff / green hair" (*ll.* 16–18); immediately, they are sexually engaged with the arrival of the sea wind, for

> the sea wind is come
> and touches them
> lightly, and strokes them, and
> screws them, until they
> are blue flames,
> green smoke, and
> screws them again.   [*ll.* 19–25]

The sea wind as "awakener" (*l.* 7) here becomes sexual aggressor, but not simply aggressor. The wind becomes both the initiator of intercourse and the result of ejaculation; this returns us to the poet-narrator's sense of transcendence, for the sea wind, as "come," is both *of* the sex act and one source (like the sea wind's emergence from the sea) of sexual pleasure. The women's transformation into "blue flames, / green smoke" suggests that certain aspects of this world contain a fluid nature that is itself as natural as the wind.

5. Denise Levertov

In the fourth variation, the last in the sequence and the longest section, the palmettos are again sexual beings, but the sea wind seems less removed from its source than it was in the previous two sections. The poet-narrator links the sea to the sea wind to the panther to the "spray inland" (*l.* 34), which makes the entire experience connective. The "shadow-colored" (*l.* 1) sea that is "without shadows" (*l.* 2) at the beginning of the poem sequence connects to the "jungle shadows" (*l.* 41) near the poem's end, as well as a "new peace / shades the mind" (*ll.* 39–40). The sea and the mountain jungles are unified in this sensual/sexual experience, and the narrator is as well. She is not merely brushed by the "silky fur" of it all, as her mind becomes part of the tapestry of the experience. Sex between jungle and sea becomes an all-encompassing sex.

The last few lines are so uniform in terms of the metaphors of the overall sequence that the reader barely notices that the poet-narrator has completely moved inside her own imagination only. All of this experience has been recreated in her psyche; she becomes tied to the external experience by her vivid internal recounting of her experience. All-encompassing sex, then, emerges from the intellect; similarly, the human body and its movements become one with the earth's movements:

> Voluptuous
>
> and simple — the world is
> larger than one had thought.
> It is a
>
> new peace
> shades the mind here
> with jungle shadows
>   frayed by the
> sea wind.   [*ll.* 35–43]

"Tomatlan (Variations)" is a work of vivid details and observations, but these observations are more "attached" to the world than detached from it, at least philosophically. In this work Levertov is neither poised to immerse herself in the Mexican culture nor poised to resist it entirely (which contains the hope for open-mindedness, at the very least).

This poem functions as a work that investigates human connections to the planet. "Levertov tries to unravel what is meant by one's 'whole space': what constitutes this space and this self? How does one exist within it, change it, understand it?" (Kinnahan 157). Space is about attachment and detachment, simultaneously, an observation that fills both the poet and the land with an inherent dynamism. Levertov rejects writing a monovocal poem, and yet it is not clear how she may move toward a polyvocal stance. Levertov's "unraveling" is the first move toward the knowledge that the "energy manifest in physical experience is also hidden within language itself; poems are therefore at least as much linguistic acts of discovery as they are discoveries of objects and forces in the 'real' world" (Breslin 154). The "new peace" in this poem confirms discovery as the result of the active poet's eye in a world of action.

Mexico's physical beauty, which "haunted her" (Rodgers 67) is portrayed as part and parcel of its sensual nature, but that nature is comparable to human nature. Mexico's topography, the sea and wind and jungles of this Pacific coast town, parallels, and even interacts, with the human body and its essential role in all of nature. This "Mexican poem," then, is not about Americanness so much as it is about "humanness." Steven Boldy tells us: "The injunction to know the other is to know oneself ... across the frontier of self " (158); similarly, Marten expounds: "Defining a sense of place and beginning to explore the ways the poet's sensibility both shapes and is shaped by it, Levertov reveals the interconnections of self and others" (9). This is a central project for this poet. Methodically, Levertov begins an investigation of such "interconnections of self and others" at its primary level: the interconnections of self and nature, "a voyage of discovery" (Rodgers 68).

Although Levertov, generally, does not advance polyvocality in her works; in the poems looked at here (which are from early in her career), this poet engages the reader in the experience of Mexico in a manner both new and different to modern readers. Her works demand that we, as readers, develop "the new sense of the listener as a partner-interlocutor" (Bakhtin, "The Problem" 66). "By the time *Here and Now* was released in 1957 and its companion volume, *Overland to the Islands*, in 1958, [Levertov] was living in the United States, and her work had already begun to show the influence of American voices and subjects" (Marten 9–10). Levertov goes on, in her career, to not only forge new "American voices and subjects," but new ways of looking and seeing experience, which Bakhtin identifies in the novel form as a "zone of maximal contact with the present (with contemporary reality) in all its openendedness" ("Epic and Novel" 11). "Contemporary reality" is, of course, unfinished and ever unfolding, an observation that requires writers and readers to be active rather than passive.

From the very first line of the poem "Overland to the Islands," Levertov as poet-narrator is grounded in the present and clearly places her reader there with her, with all its potential for "openendedness": "Let's go...." Instantly the reader is in Mexico and ready to move, indeed experience it, actively. The poem "is 'about' movement. It begins with the casual invitation 'Let's go' and then introduces the dog, as an example of movement; thereafter, poet, poem and reader move with him" (Collecott 112). This takes not only a certain level of comfort with the surroundings, but also a valuing of curiosity about places known but not yet totally known. Levertov shares the experience with her reader as we prepare to experience Mexico alongside her. Here the poem shifts almost as soon as it begins — "Let's go — much as that dog goes, / intently haphazard" (*ll.* 1–2) — and we find ourselves, along with Levertov as poet-narrator, experiencing Mexico as a dog might, closer to the ground, definitely more "intently haphazard" (*l.* 2) than a typical tourist would, in all likelihood.

Haphazardness, as a strategy, also empowers Levertov to create her own systems rather than work within prescribed masculine discourses of discovery. Kaplan suggests that:

> Recently, Euro-American feminist geographers have asked questions not only about how gender has an impact on mobility but also about how gender produces location. Such spatializations of identity and subjectivity can be interpreted as responses to the temporal accounts of modernity that cannot account for complex and differentiated subjects [Kaplan 155].

The notion of "differentiation subjects" demands an inquiry into labels by which Euro-American identities are so often simplified into simplistic categorizations. Kaplan further states that the "term 'woman' is a 'code' that cannot be confused with a generality: it has to be made into multiple particularities through temporal struggles in the spatialized embodiment of community" (175). Haphazard journeys, of most kinds, cross borders without permission or without necessarily taking seriously prescribed versions of space, time and place. In this poem, that haphazard journey belongs to the dog, as well as to the reader.

Here, what the dog experiences, we may experience. The poem itself becomes a trail of sorts. As Diana Surman Collecott states,

> One could almost say that the dog *is* the projective movement of the poem: his interest leads us from one perception to the next. Levertov has no inhibition about presenting the dog ... as a model for the poet; but nor does she attempt to press this conclusion upon us. She does not stop to do this, as she too "keeps moving" [Collecott 112–13].

Where the dog walks, we must walk:

> Under his feet
> rocks and mud, his imagination, sniffing,
> engaged in its perceptions — dancing
> edgeways, there's nothing
> the dog disdains on his way,   [*ll.* 9–13]

Note that Levertov counsels us to remain, like the dog, with our imaginations active; indeed, she reminds us to remain "engaged in ... perceptions" (*l.* 11). Clearly this falls outside of touristic space with its preplanned spectacles and exotica. Discovery, here, is about engagement of the unfolding moment; furthermore, movement is not linear from historic site to historic site, but sometimes a dance "edgeways" (*ll.* 11–12). This is quite fresh in American poetry, an invitation to experience Mexico firsthand, for ourselves, and to become lost in the experience of the moment, to see it from the perspective of one who is truly and impulsively curious. Remember: "there's nothing / the dog disdains on his way" (*ll.* 12–13).

Here Levertov is not merely relating local color, but attempting to immerse herself in the culture in new ways, with startling results; her "inspiration results not from reclusiveness but from involvement, caring involvement" (Frenkel 30). Mexico becomes another opportunity for experience, rather than something feared, foreign or fantastically other. In a move away from focusing on local color, Levertov seems to take this mission literally and infuses virtually no vivid colors in this poem; everything in the poem is earth-colored, dull, dark. The dog, the poet-narrator and ourselves remain more openended in terms of potential experience; we must abandon expectation and direction for the immediate present: "he / keeps moving, changing / pace and approach" (*ll.* 14–16), but significantly, as the poem concludes, what does not change is "direction — 'every step an arrival'" (*l.* 17). Direction then is not linear; indeed, direction breaks out of the location/dislocation dyad and becomes, instead, "arrival." Of this poem and its last line, Levertov states:

> The last phrase, "every step an arrival," is quoted from Rilke, and here, unconsciously, I was evidently trying to unify for myself my sense of the pilgrim way with my new, American, objectivist-influenced, pragmatic, and sensuous longing for the Here and Now; a living-in-the-present that I would later find further incitement to in Thoreau's notebooks ["The Sense" 69].

Significantly, the phrase "every step an arrival" reinforces Levertov's position in the here and now, as well as the poet's insistence that home is *at* hand, not the safe space behind us but a potential goal "ahead" of us (or somewhere where we will eventually arrive).

As a poet very much in multiple cultural spheres, it is clear that she is *at* home no matter where she is. Marten expounds:

> Sensitive to being partly an outsider and so seeking a place to come to, yet powerfully attuned to the physical and emotional resonances of the sensory and imaginative worlds she inhabited, Levertov made the exploration of the relation of physical to imaginative places a thematic hallmark of her verse. Placements and displacements fill the poems of her sometimes elusive highly figured British period, and

of her increasingly direct American moments, given shape in two sustained concurrent directions that her verse takes [25].

"Overland to the Islands," as an example from her American period, avoids the dichotomy of "placement and displacement" to enter another realm, what Brazilian author João Guimarães Rosa calls, in his short story by the same name, "the third bank of the river" (147). Indeed the Levertov title itself—"Overland to the Islands"—strikes critic Marten as transcendent: "If individuals want to manage creative journeys that are likely to strike the more reasonable or cautious among them as virtually impossible—over land to an island—they need not make outrageous or fantastic leaps" (36). Logic must yield to the energy inherent in discovery. Fluidity, movement, transformation, the unfolding moment all share the trait of dynamism; Richard Jackson makes the astute observation that the "final metamorphosis of metamorphosis, then, needn't be an end, but a prophecy: time becomes prophetic" (Jackson 235).

The islands, in the context of this poem, then, must be those moments of arrival; experience on the way to those moments of arrival are the steps each of us take overland "towards a final discovery" (Collecott 123). Ultimately Levertov "commends as an example for humans the forward progress of a dog" (Gitzen 127), but more importantly she refuses to distance the experience of a dog's progress in Mexico (and thus, her progress and our progress) from a dog's progress anywhere else. Like it or not, the poet-narrator in "Overland to the Islands" forces us to experience Mexico with the utmost engagement, which, in turn, insists that (human) cultural baggage be left behind. We do not have the comfort of smug judgments about much, for very little remains constant or fixed: "It is impossible to over-emphasize the activeness of Levertov's vision; she finds at the center of being, not eternal quiet, but eternal energy" (Malkoff 173). This energy cannot be contained by a poem written through a strategy of monovocality. Levertov insists that we be "intently haphazard" (*ll.* 1–2); there is room here for accidental or casual exploration.

Less "intently haphazard" is the poem "A Supermarket in Guadalajara, Mexico" with its focus on a specific location. This poem, at first, foregrounds the ordinariness of what the reader expects to follow, but Levertov elevates the ordinary into a rich, sensual realm in the course of this fifteen-line poem. "Levertov finds descriptive voice to present both exotic and fairly familiar places" (Marten 40). It is a poem of intensely vivid details and detached observations, as well as subtle moments of multi-voicing.

Rather than Mexico's physical beauty and sensual nature, to be found in poems like "Scenes from the Life of the Peppertrees," for example, here Levertov reduces the spectacular topography of Mexico to things that may be found in a Mexican supermarket, a "supermercado":

> In the supermercado the music
> >   sweet as the hot afternoon
> wanders among the watermelons,
> >   the melons, the sumptuous tomatoes,
> and lingers among the tequila bottles,
> >   rum bacardi, rompope. It
> hovers like flies round the butchers
> >   handsome and gay, as they dreamily
> sharpen their knives; and the beautiful
> >   girl cashiers, relaxed
> in the lap of the hot afternoon,
> >   breathe in time to the music
> whether they know it or not —
> >   at the glossy supermercado,
> the super supermercado.   [1–15]

Interestingly, Levertov does not insert herself, nor her readers, into the space of this supermarket, for the poet allows the music to "wander" through here, and the only people inside the poem are the "butchers" (*l.* 7) and the "girl cashiers" (*l.* 10) who are lulled by that wandering music, as well as "the hot afternoon" (*l.* 11).

Here is proof that this poet has a focused eye that almost contradictorily gazes on subjects by chance, what Gish summarizes as an "intense direct attention to her own immediate world" (257). Immediacy, even at a "glossy supermercado" (*l.* 14), offers a strategy of resistance against any restrictive masculine notions of the eternal and the seminal as qualifiers of "worthy" writings, the long or erudite poem as a worthy goal. The word choice of "glossy," itself, contains invaluable epistemological opportunities: "Her poetry may be said to be *all surface*. I have attempted to show that this is not a matter of style alone, but of the poet's state of awareness" (Collecott 122).

Although generally speaking this poem is not a work of contact, which so exemplifies the previous poem, "Overland to the Islands," neither is it a poem of disengagement. Indeed, there is much going on in these lines. Female space, and perhaps female experience, are centered in this work; thus, Levertov's poetry cannot be held up as examples of passive disengagement from the culture. Levertov here describes a sensual tableau of space, from the traditionally female-identified space of the supermarket to the sweet, rounded fruits on display to the very maternal "lap of the hot afternoon" (*l.* 11). The material realities of everyday existence contain undervalued knowledge(s). "Bodies of knowledge, physical bodies, and bodies of land coexist as subjects of feminist inquiry into the social construction of raced, gendered, sexed, and classed material life" (Kaplan 170). In Levertov, the ever-changing is what we must understand about this world before we discover it and our place(s) in it.

A poem like this one, which reverberates with the mulit-voiced moment of the mention of the Spanish word *supermercado* within the textual space of the poem, outlines the importance of including Levertov's work in this study, for here gender informs a very new look at looking and seeing culture (again that "caring involvement" [Frenkel 30]). Yet, the word *supermercado* only hints at other vocalizations that might also open up this scene from other viewpoints. For this reason, Levertov is resisting monovocality without yet moving toward a polyvocality that might end up with decentered or competing sources of voices. It is clear though that here is a poet interested in opening up, at the very least, dialogues, for conversation. Levertov explains that her works involve "a dialogue, a dialectic with everything in the world, with the self as it is projected" (Jackson 190).

As a poet engaged in craving and carving out female space in her literary works, Levertov breaks the engagement versus disengagement perspective of experiencing Mexico to allow new notions of how women see, how female observers and readers look and see, and how readers of both genders become empowered by potentially new ways of looking and seeing. Whether the girl cashiers "know it or not" (*l.* 13), and whether we, as readers, know it or not, our constructed environments — in the case of this poem the supermarket — shape our experiences "at the glossy supermercado, / the super supermercado" (*ll.* 14–15), elsewhere in Mexico or elsewhere, anywhere. Right down to the very interesting detail of "know it or not," it is clear Levertov does not impose her judgments, presumptions, etc. of what she views; as an artist with a unique identity, Levertov does not impose her perspective upon experience. Instead, she permits experience to emerge from its own constructions.

The experience that emerges from the next poem, "Scenes from the Life of the Peppertrees," is one of animation and spontaneity. The three-part poem begins on an exclamatory note: "The peppertrees, the peppertrees!" (*l.* 1). In the first section of this poem, a peppertree comes to life and appears to swallow a cat: "Robust / and soot-black, the cat / leaps to a low branch. Leaves / close about him" (*ll.* 16–19). Levertov states that this poem, as well as other of her works from the 1950s and 1960s, "may seem to have been dream-derived, but they were not. Rather they are typical examples of the poetic imagination's way of throwing off analogues as it moves through, or plays over, the writer's life" ("Interweavings" 33). Other than the detail that the peppertree is a tropical tree, this scene could be taking place anywhere.

In scene two of the "Scenes from the Life of the Peppertrees, the sound of "marimba" locates the poem more specifically in Central America or Mexico:

> Marimba
> marimba — from beyond the
> black street.
> Somebody dancing,
> somebody
> getting the hell
> outta here.   [*ll.* 22–28]

The scene here is animated, full of joy and hostility, and either emotion connotes vitality or spontaneity. Marten reminds us that Levertov "writes of space and of the people who inhabit it and discovers in the process that things are rarely only what they appear to be, even to a careful observer of the physical" (11), of which this poem is surely an example. Here the Mexicans are only present in abstract terms, as dancers or fighters. The peppertrees are more individualized, and it is their aggressive action in the third section of this poem that reinforces "that things are rarely only what they appear to be" (Marten 11).

In scene three of "Scenes from the Life of the Peppertrees," the poem centers around a sleeping man, who is not identified in terms of a husband, or a lover or a son. He is described as "defenseless ... his bare long feet together / sideways, keeping each other / warm" (*ll.* 32–35). Here the drama of the peppertrees begins anew:

> But the third peppertree
>   is restless, twitching
> thin leaves in the light
> of afternoon. After a while
> it walks over and taps
> on the upstairs window with a bunch
> of red berries. Will he wake?   [*ll.* 39–45]

"Scenes" is such an apt word for Levertov to include in her title, for this poem is clearly a drama in the process of unfolding. At poem's end, we still do not know its ending. Of this work, and the conclusion, Levertov says:

> In "Scenes from the Life of the Peppertrees" some fragment of buried myth seems to appear, when the peppertrees, graceful, modest, even diffident, but with huge gnarled roots, first swallow up among their branches a robust cat who leaps confidently into them, and then walk over and tap on the bedroom window of an innocent sleeping man, an Adam unfallen, an Abel. The purpose of the trees in attempting to waken him is not revealed.... What made me envision these trees, a species of which I am particularly fond, in this ambigu-

ous role, I have no idea — unless it was the very fact of that contrast between their graceful general appearance and their massive, knotted roots. The poem ends with the question, "Will he wake?" ["The Sense" 71].

Surely the suggestion of the sleeping man as an "Adam unfallen" reifies the concept of Mexico, or the primitive landscape, as an Edenic garden filled by innocence and abundance. Levertov, however, complicates the Adam concept with the Abel figure. Innocence and violence are again linked by the poet's mind, by the cultural myths which often are attempts at making "sense" of a sensual world. "Levertov follows Williams in a tradition of cultural revision that questions the very basis of our national mythos and its relationship to language" (Kinnahan 153); however, to end this poem with a question suggests that as poet-narrator she decenters herself.

Indeed, this landscape of peppertrees as an Edenic garden "reflects the inner experience of the speaker and is often dark, disordered by man, disturbed by ominous occurrences but always there — everlasting, perennially a reminder of nature's *ultimate* supremacy over man" (Rodgers 59). The question of whether the Adam or Abel figure, the sleeping man, may wake or not is secondary to the peppertree's intent, which may be murderous or simply natural in a cannibalistic manner, with the potential for ultimate victory. As such, Levertov connects Christian culture with primitive, mythic culture and blends them together in this Mexican Eden. "Scenes from the Life of the Peppertrees" works in a fashion similar to "Central Park, Winter, after Sunset" with its "space, or / space as dreams" (*ll.* 22–23). The "or" becomes increasingly important as Levertov's Mexico poems are juxtaposed. The poet is the bridge between spaces as realities and spaces as dreams for she has the ability and the necessity of "interlocking" many kinds of spaces. Independent from William Carlos Williams, she sees a need and an opportunity to make new lines between intellectual and geographical spaces

Levertov's last book clearly composed in the 1950s, *With Eyes at the Back of Our Heads,* was published in the first year of the new decade. Ending "with eyes at the back of our heads" seems fitting, as a concept, as the decade of the 1960s begins. Levertov's poetry collection here begins with a Toltec poem; first, it appears translated into English, titled "The Artist." Second, the Spanish translation appears, and, finally, the original in Toltec. Again, Levertov demonstrates her interest in voices, although, finally, the English translation achieves a certain authority since it is in her collection, that is the artist's "gallery." These poems are translations (and, thus, outside of the scope of this study); however, it is interesting to note that this overall poetry collection begins on such a note, which emphasizes the significant role Mexico and its cultures continually play in this poet's life: "a country whose beauty haunted her as one can see in ... *With Eyes at the Back of Our Heads*" (Rodgers 67).

In that collection, there are two original poems about Mexico, "Triple Feature" and "Xochipillil." Standing in stark contrast to the Toltec poem from an ancient codice that opens this poetry collection, Levertov takes a more modern turn by taking her readers to the movies in the poem "Triple Feature." This poem is one of the few that specifically centers Mexican people in Levertov's works. There is a couple, a husband and a wife, with a young child. As the poem begins, the couple have made a decision: an "Innocent decision: to enjoy" a movie (*l.* 1), one which just happens to be a triple feature.

It is not the movies that compose this triple feature at the center of this poem's concern, but the nobility of these three Mexicans who come from a humble station in life:

> — he in mended serape,
> she having plaited carefully
> magenta ribbons into her hair,
> the baby a round half-hidden shape
> slung in her rebozo, and the young son steadfastly
> gripping a fold of her skirt,
> pale and severe under a
> handed-down sombrero — [*ll.* 4–11]

It is within the enclosed space of two long-dashes that Levertov outlines that this couple is poor and humble, which certainly alludes to the situation of many individuals in Mexico. Through the example of this individual family, Levertov explores "'new' worlds of contact and inclusion ... reconstructing the idea of history — a history that is inclusive and immediate in each individual, private life" (Kinnahan 154); thus, through "the pathos / of hopefulness, of his solicitude" (*ll.* 2–3), this Mexican husband and father is characterized humanely. He may be poor, but he is not a person who should immediately elicit our pity. This humble family not only survives but manages to find joy.

Levertov doesn't merely look at poverty with a touristic, disengaged gaze; she sees the Mexicans and their lives as complex. Her canvas is not the two-dimensional view of foreignness or disembodied poverty, but she writes of real lives containing agency; the word choice of "solicitude" clearly underlines such agency. The lives of these Mexicans are very much like Levertov's own life, which reflects a perspective gained by long-term experience living in Mexico. This insight also offers a greater respect for humanity and a sophisticated urge to resist categorizing the Mexicans as outsiders in relationship to herself due to her own complex subject-positions "of poet, wife, mother, immigrant, and Jew (to mention a few possibilities)" (Kinnahan 129). In short, "Triple Feature" is a significant benchmark, for it presents Mexico and Mexicans as naturalized rather than as objects of fascination or pity in the stereotypical touristic gaze of either dismissal or summation, which is to Levertov's credit.

These movie-goers are observed

> ... preparing
> to pay and go in-
> to worlds of shadow-violence, half-
> familiar, warm with popcorn, icy
> with strange motives, barbarous splendors!   [*ll.* 13–17]

Unlike the Beat poets, Levertov wryly observes that the "barbarous splendor" arrives in Mexico from the modern technologies of film, those "worlds of shadow-violence." She insists that this Mexican family exists in a contemporary world, even as they also seem to exist elsewhere beyond the textuality of her poem. Just where exactly Levertov refuses to name what she sees in Mexico, rejecting the temptation to speak on behalf of the "foreigners" in their own land. Her observation of these film goers respects their positions as they encounter the "strange motives" of the modern cinema. Levertov's "attention to physical details permits [her] to develop a considerable range of poetic subject, for, like Williams, she is often inspired by the humble, the commonplace, or the small...." (Gitzen 126). Levertov isn't so much inspired by these details, but rather finds in these details the materiality that comprises many neglected histories.

Although the modernity and directness of "Triple Feature" stands in stark contrast to the Toltec poem translation that opens *With Eyes at the Back of Our Heads*, Levertov returns to the mythical with the second, and final, poem in this collection studied here: "Xochipilli." The subject of a "re-creation of ... the pre–Columbian God of Spring" (Marten 58) may well have come from an ancient codice, just as "The Artist" poem translation did. The difference is that this work is clearly Levertov's own ideas about this Mexican god.

In her essay, "The Sense of Pilgrimage," Levertov states:

> From looking at a small statue of Xochipilli, the actions of the God appeared in my mind as knowledge, rather than as uninterpreted visual images. The representation of Xochipilli, I mean, informed me of what his actions would be, and from this intuitive knowledge came visualizations and their verbal equivalents.... I cannot say that I was "steeped" in Mexican mythology. I had lived in Mexico for two years, and had read a certain amount about it and visited some of the archeological sites; however, I had no special knowledge of the attributes of Xochipilli, and did not check my intuitions against any scholarly data. Yet I feel this swiftly written little poem is an authentic revelation of the spirit of this god, transmitted to me through a representation of him made at a time when the sculptor undoubtedly believed in him as a matter of course [73–74].

Although Levertov has "no special knowledge of the attributes," Xochipilli's "actions" in the poem serve to create "an immediate evocation of the spirit of the natural world where transformations make sense beyond the rational, and nature's rhythms and sounds transfer energy to one another in a cycle of creative renewal" (Marten 58).

5. Denise Levertov

As the poem begins, the sitting figure of the god of spring is "gazing / into a fire" where "a serpent is preening, uncoiling" (*ll.* 3–5). The poem continues, with the god, the fire and the serpent remaining animated. The poem's central significance comes from what the god speaks:

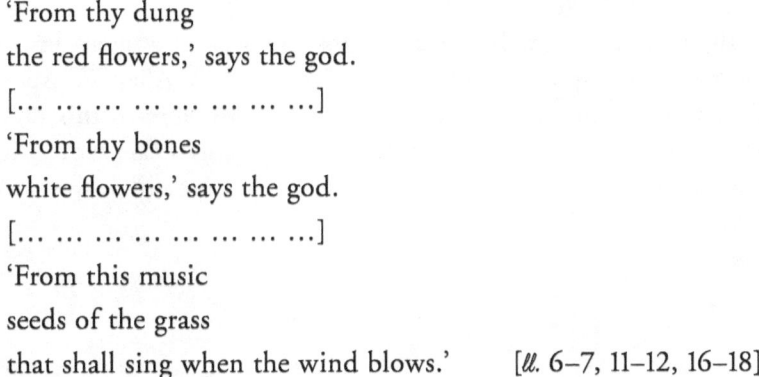

'From thy dung
the red flowers,' says the god.
[... ... ...]
'From thy bones
white flowers,' says the god.
[... ... ...]
'From this music
seeds of the grass
that shall sing when the wind blows.'   [*ll.* 6–7, 11–12, 16–18]

Each of these strophes are transformative; they defy the rational and reemphasize "a cycle of creative renewal" (Marten 58). The poem's ultimate line perfectly sums up the cyclical theme of this poem: "The god stirs the fire" (*l.* 19). Power exists in this Mexican landscape. Note again how Levertov locates a site of meaning in unexpected sources: dung and bones. The humble sources of poetry parallel the strategy deployed in the adoption of the dog's viewpoint in "Overland to the Islands."

Fecundity exists in all of nature, or at least as presented in "Xochipilli." Spring is not one phenomenon, but rather it becomes an event of multiple experiences. It is a matter of urgency to integrate these simultaneous realties, as best suggested through images, without imposing one's own will onto the landscape; "touristic are in a way semioticians, reading the landscape for signifiers of certain preestablished notions or signs" (Urry 13). Thus, this poet's touristic role is one of interpreter of all that is around her. When Levertov writes that the "god stirs the fire" (*l.* 19), conflagration and consummation aren't dissimilar fates. Here is an example of a poet who "uses the language of awe"

(Ullman 198). Awe is often beyond the power of a human being to articulate, although its representation offers a tempting challenge.

Although "Xochipilli" does not mention Mexico by name, the invocation of the Mexican god makes this poem interesting to this study. Significantly, the poem is also key to Levertov's predilection for "gods of fertility, of the natural cycle, of death as part and motive of life ... Xochipilli, for instance" (Bowering 251). Levertov remains a poet significant for her inclusion of the tapestry of ancient history, myth and contemporary realities of Mexico. Only Allen Ginsberg's treatment of Mexico in "Siesta in Xbalba" comes close to this range; however, Levertov sees beyond Ginsberg's more individual gaze of Mexico and its history and society to uncover a new, more inclusive, sense of humanity.

6

Robert Hayden

Robert Hayden's poem sequence, "An Inference of Mexico," springs from his travel experiences in Mexico in the mid–1950s after winning a Ford Foundation Fellowship for creative writing. His experiences during this period, which lasted into 1955, provide the background for the Mexican poems that he included in his poetry collection *A Ballad of Remembrance* published in 1962:

> It was a great distance that Hayden had to go in order to create his Mexican poems, but only in terms of miles. He already had the interest and the language preparation. Also, his long-standing friendship with Langston Hughes, who had spent some time in Mexico with his father, may very well have had some influence on developing his interest in the Spanish-speaking country. Hughes, together with Arna Bontemps, sponsored Hayden for a Ford Foundation Fellowship in Creative Writing that provided his sojourn in Mexico from 1954 to 1955 [P.T. Williams 92].

Hayden's interest in Spanish (he was a "Spanish major in college" [Harper 74]), which prepared him for his travels, also aided his journey that took place over "a great distance" geographically as well as intellectually and artistically. It turns out that his funded sojourn led to critical success; four years after *Ballad*, from which this poem sequence comes, Hayden was awarded the *Grand Prix de la Poésie*. Thus, "An Inference of Mexico" (a poem sequence composed of eight parts), which springs from his experiences in Mexico during this time, provides a useful site in which to look at what Hayden wants to say about Mexico, what he looks at there and also what he sees there.

Hayden takes us on an interesting journey in "Day of the Dead (Tehuantepec)," the first poem in a sequence of poems about Mexico; the reader is forced to "see" what may be recognizable to us (as gringos and outsiders); thus, we are participating in Anzaldúa's prescribed process of inevitable acceptance of both what is familiar and what at first may seem foreign to us. Hayden's poem is a "crossroads of the self" (Alarcón 47). Hayden's poem, "Day of the Dead (Tehuantepec)," as critics have pointed out previously, is a poem informed by multiple voices exterior and interior to the poet: moments of multi-voicing. This section of the study will focus particular attention on the first sequence in the poem, as it frames the rest of the poem and is the site where Hayden makes the decision to be inclusive, even as he rejects the option to speak for Mexicans. "Race is one of myriad differences that might make a human being appear alien to another, one of the assorted labels that could cause an individual to feel estranged from others as well as from himself" (Mullen 241). Rejecting the option to speak for Mexicans is a key concept as the subsequent poem sequences are examined, each of them expanding upon the foundations of polyvocality established in the first sequence. Ultimately, this is a poem about voices, about who speaks and who is being heard.

Unique to this poem when compared to other American poems that take place in Mexico in this decade, Hayden permits Mexicans to speak for themselves, within the space of the poem, "developing a poem through several speakers or voices rather than through the one voice — the one persona — that most readers expect in a poem" (S. Turner 98), which implicates "both the gaz*er* and the *gazee* in an ongoing and systematic set of social and physical relations" (Urry 145). His success on this level — and other levels in the poem sequence — may be due to multiple factors: religious affiliation, superior Spanish language skills, and most importantly, his cultural status as an outsider already, as a U.S.-born African American traveling through a racially diverse region of Mexico. This poem complicates any simple notions of foreignness, especially when place becomes a primary factor shaping a literary work.

In "Day of the Dead (Tehuantepec)," Hayden assumes the stance of a curious observer, one who watches but does not officially participate in the hope that what is "Mexican" about Mexico can emerge naturally, a position that in turn may see him as a subject of equal interest. Bakhtin reminds us that "images of language are inseparable from images of various world views and from the living beings who are their agents — people who think, talk, and act in a setting that is social and historically concrete" ("From the Prehistory" 49). Hayden's work proves he attempts to be "inseparable ... from world views" and, thus, arrives at the "social and historically concrete." Admittedly, most U.S. poets of the 1950s and their Mexican experiences captured in verse inevitably fall far short of succeeding to do this, often lapsing into a stereotypical gringo tourist, but Hayden is a refreshing exception. Here gringo is a useful term to name the typical tourist, where the baggage of ethnocentrism significantly weighs down the writer, as in the case of Jack Kerouac's *Mexico City Blues*. Hayden stands as not only a casual observer but as a careful, curious and invested observer. In "A Conversation with A. Poulin, Jr.," Hayden says "I guess I have a worldview" (30). In this case, the casual observer also happens to be an individual with a sense of cultural inclusivity.

The first section of the Hayden poem sequence stands as uniquely successful, a benchmark of cultural sensitivity for U.S. poets in the 1950s. The poem works effectively because it is not merely the narrator's internal thoughts, but a pastiche of images and polyvocal comments presented directly. Hayden avoids stereotypical gringo patterns; significantly, he does not conflate the vast country of Mexico and its diversity and avoids ignoring "the constructed nature of social reality and the historically and geographically particular nature of these constructions" (Kaplan 21). Hayden, in this poem, emerges as a poet resistant to generalizations and ethnocentric views of Mexico and Mexicans, which may be attributable to multiple factors:

> Because he could speak Spanish, Hayden was able to understand the ironic contrasts beyond the stark beauty, the harsh realities of the daily rigor. He was the outsider, the *gringo*, but he also realized one of his favorite axioms: 'No place is home for me; therefore, every place is home.' His firsthand experience of the universality of the Bahá'í was also very important to him [Hatcher 23].

While in Mexico, Hayden often stayed with fellow Bahá'ís; certainly this religious affiliation that they have in common makes differences between this particular American and the general Mexican less anxious. As Michael Harper elaborates, "Hayden has always been a symbolist poet struggling with historical fact, his rigorous portraits of people and places providing the synaptic leap into the interior landscape of the soul, where prayers for illumination and perfection are focused on the oneness of mankind" (74). This factor helps Hayden avoid arriving in Mexico with his U.S. ethnocentrism as a preconceived position. Importantly, Hayden spoke Spanish excellently, which John Hatcher emphasizes on several occasions in *From the Auroral Darkness: The Life and Poetry of Robert Hayden*. Although a thick accent and stuttering use of a foreign vocabulary may be charming to some, an obvious lack of intent to try to master the language of the host country partly typifies stereotypical gringo behavior.

Most important for this study is to keep in mind that Hayden was already an outsider, as an African American of mixed race and a "strict Baptist ... [who] later converted to Bahá'í" (Snodgrass 223) in 1950s America and "as the foster son of poor, working-class people" (Hirsch 83). Particularly in regard to the issue of mixed race, the Tehuantepec Isthmus region has a particularly intermixed — European and Indian — as well as a distinct African presence: "vestiges of African culture remain visible along the Oaxacan coast and Isthmus area" (Gutiérrez Brockington). Conceivably, then, the poet-narrator in "Day of the Dead (Tehuantepec)" is not totally excluded from the festival and the culture by the admonishing or anxious stranger in the poem because of his race and his superior language skills. There is a suggestion that some kind of a kinship exists, even if it is only a tenuous one. Typical of Hayden's poetry, "his speakers obliterate distinctions between self and other" (W. Williams 164). This poetic element helps to destabilize the presence, and centering, of Hayden; also, there is something new and powerful at work in this poem, for Hayden permits Mexicans to speak for themselves, within the space of the poem.

The narrator in this poem, apparently Hayden himself, is being spoken to by one or more strangers in a crowd; this multi-voiced text includes pieces of internalized conversation playing in the narrator's head or spoken directly to the narrator as he observes the Day of the Dead festivities. So far, critics have made no attempt to point out that these exterior voices may actually belong to more than one individual, an important distinction. In "Robert Hayden Remembered," Darwin Turner has astutely noted that Hayden "wrote many poems in which the narrator or persona strives for space with other voices" (99). This poem's details become sources of knowledge of identity as "citizen" at opportune sites for the poet. Hayden, like fellow American poet William Carlos Williams (who was half Puerto Rican), is shaped by a complex cultural citizenship, which in turn informs and shapes his gaze. Unlike Williams's "The Desert Music," another important poem about border crossing into Mexico, Hayden in "Day of the Dead (Tehuantepec)" is not reinventing himself in a Mexico made real by his own observations and intuition. Hayden sees the local and attempts to record it directly, rather than superficially looking at the local and universalizing it, forcing his readers to draw their own conclusions about the experiences at work in this poem.

The poem begins ominously with the presence of "vultures" hovering "in skies intense as voyeur's gazing" (*ll.* 1–2). The presence of these birds certainly introduces the dominant images of death early in this poem with their large, dark, cross-like bodies. Death and harshness are added to by the description of the vigorous daylight. Hayden goes on to describe the light of the day as "savage," a description which he immediately repeats as if there is no other word for it (*ll.* 6–7); thus, the day of the dead begins with a daylight that is both intensely voyeuristic and savage. This description underscores the poet-narrator's sense of his role as curious observer at the unfolding spectacle; Hayden does not appear to be participating in any kind of exchange. After all, this narrator is in a new, unknown space — Tehuantepec — and is both making sense of it and becoming sensually receptive to the unfamiliar around him in an attempt to make it more familiar.

Tehuantepec is in southern Oaxaca, which along with Chiapas, makes it one of the two southernmost Mexican states; it is on the Gulf of Tehuantepec on the Pacific. Also, the town of Tehuantepec is located on the Isthmus of Tehuantepec which is the beginning of Mexico's Yucatán Peninsula. Since it is not significantly north of the equator, even on November the second (*el Día de los Muertos*), the sky could conceivably be as hot and unforgiving as Hayden states. Indeed, in the poem, a young man solicits the attention of the poem's narrator, as they presumably stand "under palmleaf knives of sunlight" (*l.* 19). The presence of "knives" certainly suggests an exterior danger and perhaps prefigures an interior one as well.

The sky and its light is described in the first and third strophes of the poem; immediately in the second strophe, Hayden introduces us to two Day of the Dead figures, "Mr. and Mrs. Death / exposed in wedding clothes" (*ll.* 4–5). They apparently are being serenaded by "Cruciform black bells of clay" (*l.* 3). In Mexico, like many countries in Latin America, it is not unusual to find bells attached to a thick wooden yoke, in the shape of an inverted T; yoke and bell are typically attached so that they move together, as a singular unit, on an axis through the yoke. Thus, the bells appear cruciform (Bayón 26), and these are what serenade Mr. and Mrs. Death.

This is quite a striking scene in front of the narrator: cruciform bells, vultures, an intense sun, Mr. and Mrs. Death. There are images and connotations of death or mortality all around, even down to the "black clay." Notably, death here is organic and earthy; the vultures are natural, and the bells are objects made of very organic materials. The only human forms within this very natural landscape are Mr. and Mrs. Death in their wedding clothes. Interestingly, they are "exposed" (*l.* 4) within this natural, death-like topography. The ultimate human exposure is, of course to us, the skeleton; this revelation ties in neatly to Mr. and Mrs. Death and their roles on this ritualistic, celebratory holiday in Mexico.

The juxtaposition of the Death couple in their wedding clothes again serves as a startling, even surreal, image, which the Day of the Dead often is to tourists who flock to see the feasts and celebrations. This stands in contrast to Mexico's acceptance, and celebration, of death, while the United States stands, in stark contrast, as "an example of a more or less death-defying culture" (Rando 41). Although the Death couple seem exposed to the vultures, they become almost conflated with the image of the birds themselves: "The graveblack vultures encircle afternoon, / transformed by steeps of flight / into dark pure images of flight" (*ll.* 8–10); indeed, their presence is an image of imaginative flight.

Mr. Death may well be dressed in a white shirt and dark trousers, and Mrs. Death likely wears the inverse: the white of purity, innocence, birth (Covarrubias photograph 76), in opposition to the vultures. It is an arresting sight: the harsh sun, the beginning of *el Día de los Muertos*, Mr. and Mrs. Death on the street and the vultures above them with the haunting bells in the air. Hayden gazes at these forces of death all about as if they are without direct danger to him and all around him; indeed, it is a stranger in the crowd who first suggests there may be danger present. This particular Mexican holiday is such an arresting sight that until the fifth strophe of the poem we are seeing through the eyes of the narrator, without Hayden foregrounding the presence of an actual narrator in this poem.

The narrator must be as rapt as we readers are, when suddenly another voices interjects: "Such pretty girls in Juchitán, señor, / and if one desires…" (*ll.* 11–12). The narrator-listener is then transported back to the images unfolding in front of him, but the speaker's statement is not continued until the ninth strophe and not completed until the poem's end (strophes 11–12). The interjector is young and "androgynous" as he stands there talking to the narrator in a "flowered shirt"; he "invites, awaits, obliquely smiles" (*ll.* 18–20). This interruption to the narrator's attention can only be understood by the rest of his statement: "Such pretty girls, señor, / but if instead —" (*ll.* 21–22). The qualifier "but if instead" (*l.* 22) coupled with the narrator's impression of this interloper as "androgynous" can only be that this young man is offering up, or even flirting, with the presumably male narrator; the young man may here function as either a pimp or as a hustler himself. "But tourism is often about the body-as-seen, displaying, performing and seducing visitors with skill, charm, strength, sexuality and so on" (Urry 156). The observation that the young man in Hayden's poem may be offering himself sexually may not be simply an offer made for money, but clearly the proposition of pimping leads one to the more cynical view of what is being transacted here in Tehuantepec.

The sex and sexuality suggested here is a life force that informs a cultural construct of Mexico's complex relationships with the dead as a viable contrast to life; indeed, Hayden as narrator is now traveling in new country.

> Here, the advent of death looms so significantly in the peon's life that a special day is set aside in observation of it. Death can be, he says, as commonplace for them as is the candy.... On the other hand, it could be the 'error' of the peon's spiritual death and degradation through male and female prostitution that overwhelms the poet-observer.... Here, Hayden demonstrates discerning realism and perceptiveness in his treatment of the morally stultifying tentacles that, in his view, have sprung from the peon's economic plight. This dimension of his literary concern, first focused on ghetto blacks, then, successfully, on poor whites, Jews, and European war victims, firmly emphasizes, in *A Ballad of Remembrance*, his thematic stance on the oppressed of all nations. It is a stance that indicts the oppressors and it is one from which Hayden does not waver in his subsequent volumes [P.T. Williams 95–96].

Against this backdrop, in the poem sequence of "An Inference of Mexico"—from which this individual poem comes—it may be easier for the critical reader to see the sexual innuendoes as economic in origin and degrading as a result of economic conditions. Typically, "there are usually enormous inequalities between the visitors and the indigenous population, the vast majority of whom could never envisage having either the income or the leisure time to be tourists themselves" (Urry 52). The idea of sexual and/or economic degradation in P.T. Williams's quote reveals as much of American morality as it does about Hayden's refusal to flinch in this poem. Here in the context of this particular poem, it may be simply a life-affirming offer of sex that stands in contrast to the celebration at hand, with its backdrop of death. This latter interpretation returns a realistic sense of agency to this provocative, young man (perhaps a pimp or a hustler).

In any case, the interaction seems casual, everyday and realistic; however, the realism dramatized here also proves to be complex, for nothing remains here as either simplistic or static. Instead, oppression of all sorts may lead to sexuality as a site of resistance, of a closing down of borders. Torgovnick reminds us that "global politics, the dance of colonizer and colonized, becomes sexual politics, the dance of male and female" (17). Without a doubt the sexual economy of Mexico's tourism, like tourism globally, has always depended a great deal on women, and men, making its citizens sometimes available to the sexual whims of tourists. Snodgrass, for one, has also suggested that some of Hayden's poem "allude to a bisexual condition" (223). As for the speaker in the poem, we must keep in mind that sexual acts, particularly under third-world economic pressures, is not always a concrete, static qualifier of one's actual sexual orientation.

The young man's remarks to the narrator are suggestive, perhaps more so if they are the last words he speaks: "but if instead —" (*l.* 22). The way it stands here seems to be an open-ended come-on of some sort, an invitation for the curious observer to become a prying observer (or voyeur) by naming himself, by facing up to his own wants and desires, perhaps for Hayden, "a thoughtfully religious man struggling to reconcile his sexuality with his spirituality" (Mullen 240) (the Bahá'í religion, like many world religions, upholds heterosexuality as "the norm" and frowns upon sexual "deviation"). In any case, the poem's final two strophes, three lines long, can be read as the completion of this androgynous stranger's train of thought. The text, again, shifts its left margin, as when the young man speaks to the narrator. The "Day of the Dead (Tehuantepec)" poem ends: "Flee, amigo, for the dead are angry; / flee, lest the hands of dead men strike us down, / and the vultures pick our bones" (*ll.* 26–28). Note how the tone here is different. Has the narrator rebuffed him, causing this transition? Possibly. Or are these internalized thoughts going on in the narrator's head? Perhaps another stranger, a third voice, hearing or intuiting the young man's suggestions to the narrator, is admonishing him to some extent by posing the threat: "Flee ... for the dead are angry" (*l.* 26). Does this poem end, then, with a warning that a sexual crossing will not be tolerated by the living or the dead? Possibly, but it does definitely end with a warning implicating the spectator (in this case Hayden as narrator) to the death spectacle. "Because of the importance of the visual, of the gaze, tourism has always been concerned with spectacle and with cultural practices which partly implode into each other" (Urry 78); Hayden, as narrator, appears to be invited to involve himself directly with the Day of the Dead events, those visible to the reader (and narrator) and those less than visible to us.

Clearly the statements in Hayden's poem that do not belong to the narrator are structured as if a Mexican speaks them; the use of the Spanish word "amigo" reinforces that, but they are not stated exclusively by the one young stranger. Again, in Hayden's poetry, the "reader must distinguish the voices by the subject, the diction, the language, or the tone" (D.T. Turner 99). Earlier in the poem, in the third strophe, it reads: "Savage the light upon us, / savage the light" (*ll.* 6–7), which then must also be the young man's words or another stranger's words. Either the young man speaks all the words which shift in the left margin, or only some of those words, but clearly here, too, the use of the word "us" makes it clear that it is not merely the narrator's internal thoughts. If all those strophes which shift to the left margin are attributed to the young man, then the rest of the text remains mere observation, impression, an attempt to observe. That seems feasible for Hayden. Indeed, he may be attempting to capture an experience "objectively," journalistically (the role of a curious observer). Reginald Gibbons reminds:

> Never an effusive poet, always spare and precise, working to control the emotional response that a poem realizes, Hayden at moments of greatest intensity will cut back to the sparest lines of all, letting an image — in the purely visual sense — stand for everything he does not wish to state explicitly. "Kodachromes of the Island," a poem that is one version of a poetic impulse Hayden seems to have honored more than once ("An Inference of Mexico," "Islands," for example) is characteristic [217–18].

Photographic journalism, like print journalism, is steeped in the tradition of objectivity. Detached observations are at the heart of this ... philosophy, especially "spare and precise" observations.

If we skip over or ignore the "stranger's"— or strangers'— words from this poem, then what frames these strangers' interjections are detached observations that begin in the first two lines of the poem:

"The vultures hover wheel and hover / in skies intense as voyeur's gazing" (*ll.* 1–2). What follows are details about Mr. and Mrs. Death, the vulture, the children playing "with Jack-in-the-tomb and skulls of marzipan" (*l.* 15), the androgynous young man and, finally, "Barefoot Tehuanas in rhythmic jewels of gold [who] / bear pails of marigolds upon their heads / to the returning dead" (*ll.* 23–25). Clearly it reads like an actual experience; the observations are presented directly, the unfolding moment in all of its details. Stated this way, everything here appears to be the narrator's, or Hayden's, observations. The details are presented in the order in which the narrator's eye catches them (even down to the "marigolds," the "*cempoalxochitl* [the orange flower of the dead]" that are used to create paths from the graves to their homes "so that the souls may find their way to the offerings" (Lomnitz-Adler 215). They are local color, yes, but the narrator does not appear to overemphasize the exoticism of the festival and, instead, records the striking details in front of him as important, worthy.

What is stated to the narrator (located outside of his own observations) is interesting to analyze, for this is where observation yields to engagement. For the sake of structure and clarity here, let me divide what is conversational within the poem into two sections; the first section, what I call the "young man" section, is that which the androgynous, young man directly states to the poem's narrator:

> Such pretty girls in Juchitán, señor,
> and if one desires —....
> Such pretty girls, señor,
> but if instead —   [*ll.* 11–12; 21–22]

The second section, possibly spoken by "another stranger," may also be the continuation of the words spoken by the first young man, but noticeably they are clearly outside the context of the former come-on; these lines may be said by the young man — in a radically different tone — or by one or more other strangers:

> Savage the light upon us,
> savage the light....
> Flee, amigo, for the dead are angry;
> flee, lest the hands of dead men strike us down,
> and the vultures pick our bones   [*ll.* 6–7; 26–28]

In the "young man" section, the man issues a sexual come-on, in the role of a pimp or the role of a sexually available individual himself.

On one level, the young man is simply pointing out the beauty of the girls in this particular part of the country: "Such pretty girls in Juchitán, señor.... / Such pretty girls, señor" (*ll.* 11, 21). Interestingly, this conversation is taking place in the town of Tehuantepec, not nearby Juchitán; and, obviously part of the subtext here is town rivalry. Indeed, a "review of the history of Juchitán and Tehuantepec will show that the roots of the mutual hatred between the two towns are deep-set and unavoidable" (Covarrubias 160). Perhaps by going to Juchitán, Hayden's narrator will arrive at an even more interior and "unknown" Mexico, but that does not come to pass within this poem. Still, the invitation stands and engages the narrator's attention, if not interest.

The more interesting elements of the young-man section are the two lines: "and if one desires —.... / but if instead —" (*ll.* 12, 22). Both of these lines function as qualifiers; both are qualifiers in relation to the "pretty girls" of the area. These lines, obviously, are almost repetitive, but with an important difference. That difference hinges upon everything that is implied by the contrast(s) between "and" and "but," as well as the words "one desires." Also of interesting contrast is the inclusivity of the first statement ("and if one desires" [*l.* 12]) and the exclusivity of the second statement ("but if instead" [*l.* 22]).

Here the young Mexican may or may not be including the narrator as an insider in the festivities and the culture, but he is attempting to include the narrator in sex, either with the young girls (or boys) or himself. Hayden apparently does not pass judgment on either of these desires. ("Though he was a devoted husband and father, some cryptic poems allude to a bisexual condition" [Snodgrass 223].) Whether this has anything to do with this poetic moment or not, the use of the word "and" functions to emphasize that the girls are not only pretty, but available; in the young man's next strophe, the use of the word "but" functions to emphasize that if the narrator's sexual orientation may be homosexual, that he himself or other men are available. Possibly the poet-narrator is unaware of the suggestion(s) because he does not respond, but that seems unlikely for he is an astute observer up to this point. The narrator does not appear to respond to the young stranger; in fact, he registers neither interest nor disgust, but continues to remain a distant but curious observer.

The young man and possibly the "other stranger" are going outside themselves to engage the poem's observer, whether for economic gain or sexual gain, or whether to simply offer a stern warning. Indeed the speaker other than the young man is not explicitly propositioning this tourist for anything. It remains the young man only who engages the narrator in sexual matters. Although the young man may have been forced to prostitute himself or the young girls in a nearby town, he may also be seeking escape from the hyper-awareness of death, which is all around them. In that case, he may be engaging the narrator as an equal in this spectacle, transcending "the space between self and other" (W. Williams 163). At this moment in the poem, this may be queer desire, or this may be simply life-affirming desire, or perhaps both.

Again, inherent in the concept of the Day of the Dead is a contrast between elements of the life-affirming and death-affirming. Another contrast in this work is that Hayden often contrasts social reality against "Mexico's awesome natural beauty — the beauty that the rich *turista* comes to see and enjoy" (P.T. Williams 93). Viewing physical beauty, as well as experiencing sensual beauty, are both remarkable contrasts to actual and documentable poverty and mortality. Separating them is to deny the day-to-day effects of oppression: "Hayden, as the outsider observing a sort of grim gaiety, notes the way in which the floral sensuousness of the celebrants competes in a desperate contrast with death's harsh reality. Vultures 'hover...,' just as the past hovers over the present" (Fetrow 85). Future death hovers over this poem's present as well (as mortality always does), and sex or sensual play is one celebratory (and temporary) escape from that reality. Because the young man possibly offers up homosexual desire in addition to, or as an alternative to, heterosexual desire, this does not immediately taint this scene as one of degrading or demeaning prostitution. Throughout the larger sequence, "An Inference of Mexico," Mexican individuals struggle to survive, in sometimes illegal manners, but there are also Mexicans who indulge in joy and an acceptance of unregulated behavior. Just as the spectacle of death in this Mexican festival is a reminder to live fully, John Hatcher reminds us that this individual poems recalls "the Keatsian fascination for death as a vitalizing transcendence" (135). Hayden's poem, like the celebration of the Day of the Dead, becomes as much about the living, which many tourists fail to recognize.

If we look at everything "spoken" to the narrator that may not be spoken by the young man, the "other stranger" section, there is not only a profound shift in tone but a different sort of inclusivity at work. Inclusivity may not be the most accurate word to describe what is taking place, for the narrator is *not* directly being excluded from the festivities or the culture. The lines of the poem we are left with, first of all, seem quite unified in tone; they are harsh, almost admonishing:

Savage the light upon us,	[*l.* 6]
savage the light.	[*l.* 7]
[... ... ...]	
Flee, amigo, for the dead are angry;	[*l.* 26]
flee, lest the hands of dead men strike us down,	[*l.* 27]
and the vultures pick our bones.	[*l.* 28]

The two strophes spoken by the young man, like these strophes, are remarkably unified in their tones. The stranger in the poem (who speaks the lines above), very likely is one other individual, one who sounds anxious or fearful (perhaps even more experienced and realistic), as well as judgmental. It appears, then, that this portion of the poem is truly spoken by a person other than the young man who propositions the narrator.

We find the stranger including the narrator in his or her own anxieties and fears. The use of "us" in each of the two strophes and the use of "our bones" in the final line each implicate the narrator in this speaker's psychic state. The "us" that is spoken may not be an indication that Hayden is mistaken for a fellow Mexican, but there is some validity that he is a more a "friend" than a foe. The entire poem sequence underscores a more unique inclusivity by a poet writing about Mexico than in works by any other major U.S. poet writing about Mexico in the 1950s. Hayden is both a curious observer and a subject of curious (perhaps prying) observance. These poems offer the reader what Bakhtin terms in language collision "interillumination" ("From the Prehistory" 49). Here the Others are African Americans and Mexicans who become visible to each other; their citizenships are complex, something beyond a passport's official discourse. In this particular poem, Hayden is not instantly distanced as a gringo, a position that his racial identity possibly contributes to; another contribution may be that he observes but shows no explicit judgment on anything displayed before him or offered to him.

Even if what the Mexicans say isn't particularly definitive or climactic, this poet-narrator sees, and hears, but he does not appear to judge. More importantly, he does not paraphrase the statements made to him, but allows them to stand, seemingly, on their own words.

> Regardless of the cause, the fact is that Hayden not only wrote many poems in which the narrator or persona strives for space with other voices, but Hayden even required the reader to identify the different speakers as one might listening to a drama on radio. The reader must distinguish the voices by the subject, the diction, the language, or the tone [D.T. Turner 99].

Mexicans speaking within U.S. poetry is new space here. "The dominant theme in Hayden's Mexican poems seems to be the reality which lies behind Mexico's appearance" (P.T. Williams 92).

Hayden is a cultural and political hybrid, for he chooses to decenter himself in Mexico to see what emerges within the culture, as if his particularities can be put aside. Yet obviously his status as a U.S. minority allows him to see those who may also be characterized as outsiders or foreigners. By standing back and trying to observe objectively, by allowing Mexicans to speak from their own experiences, Hayden is trying to be "sensitive to the implications of history" (Fetrow 85). This sensitivity is summed up as:

> First, because the poet wanted to express the spirit of Mexican culture, rather than just reproduce picturesque detail, the work shows his strong sense of history. He recurrently emphasizes his sense of how, in Mexico, the past is everywhere dramatically tangible in the present. Second, and typically, Hayden's fascination with humanity, beyond fact or artifact, causes many of his Mexican scenes to be filled with living presences, ghosts of the past and contemporary "natives" affected by the impact of their cultural history [Fetrow 85].

Although the Day of the Dead's ritualized promotion of contact with the dead (Walter 118) may not be completely familiar to Hayden, for African Americans generally, as for Mexicans, "poor people constantly come into contact with death because their poverty puts them in continual jeopardy.... When we are more familiar with something, we are more accepting of it" (Younoszai 70).

This contact with the dead does not respect geopolitical borders, but it is also not a space that opens to everyone. Indeed, Barbara Younoszai states it most bluntly when she says, "Death, then, is present everywhere in Mexico.... And it must always be included as a part of the Mexican reality" (76). Hayden's poetic depiction of the Day of the Dead, while culturally specific, is an opportune site of his "fascination with humanity" (Fetrow 85). However, for many Americans in mid-century and even up to the present, there is no fascination with this unique holiday; there is often only fear or ignorant disdain.

In turn, the strangers at this Mexican festival do not exclude, or dismiss, the narrator as a mere tourist or gringo. One stranger introduces sexual opportunities to the narrator, and the other stranger gives a sort of communal warning to the observer during one of Mexico's most spectacular holidays: *el Día de los Muertos*. It is a festival where the calendar of the living and the timeless dead collide, a site of fluidity and redefinitions. This Day of the Dead to Mexicans (and to many Latinos) becomes about the living, which many gringos fail to recognize; Hayden provides us this opportunity to encounter the holiday in a poem that begins as a distanced experience but ends as one about the invisible forces that shape what is ultimately seen. The curious observer of this festival learns as much about the living as he does about the dead.

The poet-narrator functions less as a typical "outsider" in this culture because he is accustomed to standing in marginalized positions. Here, Anzaldúa reminds us that those "who are pushed out of the tribe for being different are likely to become more sensitized (when not brutalized into insensitivity)" (38). Also, Hayden's religious status, his superior language skills in Spanish, and his unique position as a U.S.-born African American traveling in a racially diverse region of Mexico help shape this important poem.

After the first section, Hayden has successfully articulated his interests within the longer poem: polyvocality, the sexuality of the festivities and culture, as well as death and life as the two vital forces of this world. These insights are tempered by the limits of one overall narrator; Hayden's Mexico is and isn't his. Yet the daily realities of what can be observed and experienced prevent Hayden from emptying the images and experiences of Mexico of their historical materiality. The subsequent poems that comprise the larger project build upon these insights, as Hayden foregrounds the process of making sense of the foreign even as he comes to respect what isn't his at all. We witness Hayden grapple with history, the tourist's gaze and the constant presence of death, among other themes. Each poem is set apart with its own title, although clearly they are linked by the one holiday under observation; however, each section is an individual experience.

"Mountains," the second section of the poem sequence, is short, merely six lines long. At first it appears to be simply imagistic, in a photographic sense, but the mountains that form this section's title are not static images. Indeed, this small poem is animated, but that animation completely rests upon the last line, where noise potentially may bring action from the gods. Unlike the poem sections that precede it and follow it, there are no people present in the three-strophe section, no Mexicans and no poet-narrator, although both are somewhat present in their absences.

A work this short, typically, depends upon what it excludes as well as what it includes. In short, things sometimes become present through absence. Hayden also seems to agree with P.T. Williams that there is truth in the notion that meaning "depends" on what appears unimportant; marginalized individuals often are aware of how details may create compelling commentaries on institutionalized systems. One of the more interesting facets to this short poem section is how Hayden centers the potential for animation, for kinesis.

First the reader may notice how the structure of the first strophe is passive, which is reinforced by the use of the past tense. Also, the impacted metaphor of "Dark as if cloven from darkness" (*l.* 1) adds to the almost claustrophobic structure here. The second strophe functions much the same; "Night-angled fold on fold" (*l.* 3) is impacted similarly. Although the structure of this strophe is also in the past tense, it is not written in the passive voice. This gives the reader a hint of change, a hint that a potential dynamism from the past may reoccur or, at the very least, provide commentary on the present. Again, these mountains are centered, but here we begin to get a glimpse of "sunlight" (*l.* 4) through the "mist" (*l.* 4), which begins to bring us out of the darkness.

Darkness, again, emerges in the first line of the third strophe. The mountains are described as possessing "surging darkness" (*l.* 5); note how here, instead of, or in addition to, darkness, mist or sunlight, Hayden suddenly centers sounds. Out of the "surging darkness" (*l.* 5) comes "drums bells gongs" (*l.* 6), but these words function less as nouns than as verbs (verbs, noticeably, in the present tense). From such "drums bells gongs" (*l.* 6) comes entreatment; finally, the sounds implore "a god" (*l.* 6). It seems this works in a tradition of the creation myth; first there is nature epitomized by mountains, and then there is a god. The suggestion is that humans may follow, participating in the ever present world.

Out of nature, out of passivity and darkness comes sun and life; the mountains bring a god into being. Ultimately, this small poem is a profound statement on change, on creation. This is part of the canvas of a history of Mexico that precedes nation; it reaches to the base of a place, and possibly, a people who may come to inhabit such a place. The personal narrative has yielded to an accounting of mythic dynamism. Even something as solid as a mountain is more than its materiality; Hayden transforms it into a metaphor of kinesis.

The third poem in the sequence, "Veracruz," is, itself, subdivided into two sections. Like the first section of "An Inference of Mexico," it is casual observation of ordinary life in Mexico. As the poem begins, it could be a scene from almost anywhere taking place on a "Sunday afternoon," as the first line states. Slowly the details emerge, which place this scene in Mexico, keeping in mind that the poem section is titled specifically "Veracruz." It is clear that this is a place by the sea, where "Indian boys idle and fish" (*l.* 5); and, a "shawled brown woman / [squints] against the ricocheting brilliance / of sun and water" (*ll.* 6–8). In the distance, on the horizon, is an old Spanish fort, a "fossil" of imperialism (*ll.* 11–12) "looming in the harbor" (*l.* 13).

Suddenly, the poem pits the beauty of the sea and the seashore against the stark reality of human survival: "a temple ... hides the inward-falling slum / the stains and dirty tools of struggle" (*ll.* 15–20). Hayden, as poet-narrator, states: "Here only the sea is real" (*l.* 23), but in the two consequent strophes, another voice is interjected into the poem. Distinctly set apart by italics, the seven lines do not appear to be a strategy similar to that used in the first poem in the sequence. Rather this is a voice with a prophetic pronouncement, a Bakhtinian moment of interillumination:

> *Leap now*
> *and cease from error.*
> *Escape. Or shoreward turn,*
>
> *accepting all—*
> *the losses and farewells,*
> *the long warfare with self,*
> *with God.* [*ll.* 30–36]

It adds a philosophical tone to the work, but also returns the reader to the theme that emerged in "Day of the Dead (Tehuantepec)." It stresses the personal and cosmic conflict or struggles between life and death, which is more obviously foregrounded in Mexican culture than in U.S. culture. Even in the lines quoted above, note how "the long warfare with self" (*l.* 35) takes place in the seascape and landscape of Veracruz.

Hayden concludes part one of "Veracruz" by returning to the sea, as if such meditations are worthy of being voiced but not dwelled upon for long, for there may be no answers to such questions. Part two of this third poem in the overall sequence does not so much begin a new thought as sum up the part preceding it; the second part of "Veracruz" begins: "Thus reality" (*l.* 42). Reality, Hayden tells us here, becomes "unbearably a dream" (*l.* 49), which is "out of reach" (*l.* 51). Just then Hayden returns to the word "thus" again, as if arriving at a second, possibly different, conclusion; this time, the night and the sea "become phantasmal / space" (*ll.* 56–57) until finally, as Hayden concludes "Veracruz," "one farewell image / burns and fades and burns" (*ll.* 58–59), but at this point it is not clear what that image may be. Veracruz, as a real geopolitical site, coexists with the "phantasmal / space" all about it. The poet is not emptying the site by making it an ahistorical mythic city, as Ginsberg has often been tempted to do. Rather, Hayden sees the potentiality of the abstract and the eternal as a potentiality within the actual.

Seemingly, the image that ends the previous poem leads us toward the next work in the sequence, "Idol (Coatlicue, Aztec goddess)." This sequence is the darkest and rawest section of the poem sequence. From the "[w]ail of the newborn, cry of the dying" (*l.* 1), all "agonies" (*l.* 2) in this poem lead to the apparent, human sacrifice: "the raw meaty heart quivering in copal / smoke its praise" (*ll.* 7–8). There is human life in this poem and human suffering; there is death, which may force us to escape into a life lived more fully, at best, and then there are powers greater than humans. As Hayden told A. Poulin Jr. in regard to Octavio Paz and what has been generally written and stated about Mexico, "the old Gods, the old Aztec gods, the old Toltec Gods, are still around; they haven't died" (Hayden, "A Conversation" 40). Whether it is such a powerful old god or the sheer power of the sea, in the scope of this poem it is a force that may cause suffering and grief, but it, itself, is a power greater than human suffering. It is a source of oppression but also symptomatic of natural conditions or forces. In the sense the force may be brutish and inevitable, the Mexicans have, partly, inherited suffering from their ancestors, but Hayden does not permit this conclusion to remain that simplistic, that static.

The violence of the Aztec goddess, Coatlicue, stands next to the allusions to the Spanish conquest in the preceding poem. Also, Coatlicue becomes almost conflated with the violent and beautiful sea in the former poem sequence. By charting a sense of human fate along a triad, Hayden further pushes his analysis beyond overt simplifications. In short, Hayden brings complex critique to bear upon Mexico, Mexicans, their contemporary history, as well as colonial and ancient histories. As poet-narrator in "An Inference of Mexico," Hayden refuses to simply look at situations and experiences and begin to draw superficial conclusions; he is a curious observer who attempts to maintain an objective stance. In fact, he assumes that what makes up Mexico is as complex — or more complex — than what makes up the United States, for example. He sees deeply into the culture. Hayden avoids speaking on behalf of others and refuses to simplify what he observes. Instead he writes of the land's effect and people's effect on his own psyche; his interpretations reveal as much about his own mindset as they do about what his mind has taken in.

The graphic human sacrifice of "Idol (Coatlicue, Aztec goddess)," the fourth poem in the sequence, becomes flattened in the fifth section, "Sub Specie Aeternitatis," a poem Hayden admits to A. Poulin Jr. as being inspired by "a visit to a Mexican convent in Tehuacán" (Hayden, "A Conversation" 39). Here Hayden describes empty Aztec temples and empty Catholic convents, which have now become mere tourist sites. These

> curious
> may walk the cloister now,
> may enter portals barred
>   to them no longer
>   and wander
> hidden passageways and rooms
> of stone, meditating on
>   such gods as they possess,
>   as they have lost.   [*ll.* 13–21]

"Sub Specie Aeternitatis" ends "resonant with silence of / a conquered and / defiant god" (*ll.* 28–30). Again, there is animation here, although it is subdued animation lurking just slightly behind superficial stasis. This is a remarkable move away from descriptions that seem merely postcard-like; underneath the apparent loss, there is still hope and potential action. It is as if this is Hayden's statement about Mexico, its bloody history and conquest by Spain, its modern political system(s), underclass and political corruption; under all the negative, there thrives a vital and still-defiant nation and culture.

There is a sense of perspective being offered in the lines "curious / may walk the cloister now" (*ll.* 13–14). The "now" is important, for it suggests a safe position from which to look at the past and all of its harshness. The notion that gods can be lost, a paraphrase of lines 20–21, is apparently a frightening one. Only by stepping outside of the normalized and dominant structures of knowledge can one clearly see how Hayden's "hidden passageways and rooms" (*l.* 18) also hide the metasystems of social and cultural hegemony. Looking at the past not only informs Hayden (and his readers) of how the present may have been influenced by it, but also how we may be similarly myopic about our own systems and "such gods as they possess" (*l.* 20).

In the next two poems, "Market" and "Kid (Cuernavaca)," a certain sense of "defiance" emerges. In "Market," Mexico's ragged, begging boys and other realities of a Mexican marketplace stand in opposition to the rich, spoiled tourists. In this poem, the poet-narrator makes some of his strongest comments on the touristic gaze. Hayden's observations mingle with the forthright reflections on tourists and their attitudes; polyvocality is at play here, as Mexicans' thoughts mingle with the thoughts of Hayden. He writes:

> Turistas pass.
> Por caridad, por caridad.
> Lord, how they stride
> on the hard good legs
> money has made them.
> Ay! you creatures
> who have walked
> on seas of money all
> your foreign lives!
> Por caridad.   [*ll.* 23–32]

Clearly the word choice of "turistas" prevents the poem from being monovocal; furthermore, the expression "Por caridad"—repeated three times—disrupts the poet-narrator's objective narrative. It locates not only the particularity of the Mexican marketplace, but reveals a Bakhtinian link

> toward the response of the other (others), toward his active responsive understanding, which can assume various forms: educational influence on the readers, persuasion of them, critical responses, influence of followers and successors, and so on. It can determine others' responsive positions under the complex conditions of speech communication in a particular cultural sphere. The work is a link in the chain of speech communion ["The Problem" 75–76].

Such a Bakhtinian "link in the chain of speech communion" (76) reappears in the next poem, as well. Note how the "turistas" are the ones suddenly described as having "foreign lives" (*l.* 31), an inversion of the tourists calling locals "foreigners" in their own land. Hayden locates the tension between the foreign and the non-foreign in terms of economic superiority or domination. These "turistas" walk "on seas of money" (*l.* 30), a wry satire of the Biblical tale of Christ walking on the water. Clearly Hayden does not side with his fellow visitors to Mexico; he has managed to find a position in which to view the comic and yet tragic theater of capitalism on an equal basis with the Mexicans, who may or may not themselves be struggling to survive in third-world poverty.

In "Kid (Cuernavaca)," the seventh poem in the sequence, Hayden gives us an intimate look at one of the boys in the marketplace which he introduced in the last poem; amidst the poverty of contemporary Mexico that is this boy's reality, the "kid" utilizes stereotypical touristic empathy. Hayden writes:

> Tricks of pathos for
>   the silly foreigners
> and so manages not to starve.
>   Waiters strike at him and curse;
> Deft and quick and accustomed,
>   he dances beyond their blows,
> taunts them and scampers off,
>   laughing as he goes. [*ll.* 5–12]

Clearly, here, the poet-narrator does not simply look at the boy and the conditions which lead him to play tricks on the tourists, but Hayden goes beyond that. He sees the situation from the boy's point of view; he is anything but a victim, which the ultimate line reiterates. Note how the "waiters strike at him and curse" (*l.* 8) thus implicating other Mexicans in the attempted domestication and homogenization of even a beggar boy; Hayden here is not making simple distinctions between tourists and non-tourists.

This boy has agency, for he outwits a system that views him with "pathos" (*l.* 5) by using that very system to his advantage. Resisting the tourists, and their preconceptions of him and his culture, the boy uses his performance as a matter of practicality (money) and critique ("the silly foreigners" [*l.* 6]). He is not an object of the reader's pity, but a victorious character whose own self-satisfaction we have to applaud.

Finally, "An Inference of Mexico" ends on a very nationalistic note with the eighth, and last, poem in the sequence: "La Corrida" (the bullfight). Subdivided into three parts, Hayden labels them: "El toro" (the bull), "el matador" (the bullfighter — literally, the killer) and "sol y sombra" (sun and shade). The bullfight is offered as a synecdoche of Mexico itself, in its theater of violence and as a symbolic struggle of forces.

In the first part of the poem, "El toro," Hayden interestingly characterizes the bull as: "Man-in-beast" (*l.* 5), but a "creature / whose guileless power is his doom" (*ll.* 5–6). Because of this particular characterization, it is unclear if it is the man in the phrase "man-in-beast" or simply the beast with the "guileless power" (*l.* 6) who is "guileless"; if it can be read both ways, then Hayden's concept of man here seems aligned with Christian, and Bahá'í, notions of humankind's incidental fall from grace, as well as the sanctity of animals' lives which Bahá'ís attempt to honor by being vegetarians. In this part of the poem, the bull — whose "horns are law" (*l.* 2) — "enters the clockface labyrinth" (*l.* 4) where the bullfighter waits for him "[i]n the heart of the maze" (*l.* 7). The second strophe of the "El matador" part of the poem begins: "The fateful one, fate's dazzler" (*l.* 11), but it is unclear who is who here. Is the "fateful one" the one who "gleams in suit of lights, / prepares for sensual death / his moment of mocking truth" (*ll.* 12–14) the bullfighter? It seems likely, since this part of the poem "La Corrida" is called the bullfighter, but is the bullfighter, then, also the "fateful one" who dies as he dazzles fate (*l.* 11)? The ambiguity suggests that both the bullfighter and the bull, as opposing systems, are so linked together that they cannot be usefully separated one from another.

The "matador" part of "La Corrida" ends: "In the fiery heart of the maze / the bullgod moves, / transfiguring death / and the wish to die" (*ll.* 15–18). Any guesses as to the nature of the scenario unfolding before our (readerly) eyes is nebulous, at best. Are the bull and bullfighter both wounded? Is one or the other, or both, dying? Perhaps the only key this poem holds lies in the third part of "La Corrida"; "Sol y sombra," which concludes the overall poem sequence, contains the most philosophical lines in "An Inference of Mexico." In its entirety, the "sun and shade" part reads:

>From all we are yet cannot be
>deliver, oh redeem us now.
>Of all we know and do not wish
>to know, purge oh purge us now.
>
>   Olé!
>
>Upon the cross of horns
>be crucified for us.
>
>Die for us that death
>may call us back to life.
>
>   Olé!   [*ll.* 22–31]

The bullfight becomes an arena for theological concerns, a tidy summary of human "wishes" to defeat death through some kind of redemption. James Emanuel points out that "the final stanza of 'La Corrida' [exemplifies] technical, emotional, and philosophical richness" (63). Hayden concludes this sequence of poems with this work as a means to universalize his Mexico experiences, but his universalization does not reject Mexico and the Mexican people's particularities and agency. Rejecting the power of ventriloquism (speaking for others), Hayden can now join others in a new performance, similar to that in the previous poem. This time though, it is not one boy who speaks, but rather an arena of people unified in one voice: "Olé" (*ll.* 5, 10). It is a living version of "Amen," as individuals volunteer to speak as one. By evoking the crucifixion, presumably of Christ, Hayden has grafted his theological interests along with the more ancient notions of sacrifice (particularly Aztec sacrifice). The "us" in line 9 is an earned moment of inclusivity. Rather than speaking for others, Hayden has found a site in which all volunteer to speak the same word at the same time.

Other critics have found much power in this sequence of poems, many of them remarking on Hayden's interests beyond the aesthetic. A good example of this kind of commentary is by Pontheolla Williams:

> The dominant theme in Hayden's Mexican poems seems to be the reality which lies behind Mexico's appearance. The worst dimension of what he perceives to be Mexico's reality is the stultifying condition of poverty there that either shrouds the victims with apathy or reduces them to a demeaning scramble for subsistence. He reveals these perceptions in what he sees as Mexico's toleration of public begging and prostitution, its preoccupation with death, and its acceptance of poverty as a way of life for many of its citizens [92–93].

What P. Williams doesn't address is that Hayden is doing more of a sociological history of Mexico or perhaps producing some kind of documentary. He has chosen to write of many Mexicos through the genre of poetry, an interesting and original challenge. By admitting other voices in his poems, Hayden cautiously works toward the possibility that we may be linked as human beings, no matter our class positions and investments in nationalism. Sexual difference, theological systems of the past and the present and economic inequalities encourage Hayden to admit that the world is more complex than any one simple aphorism or parable might pretend to sum up.

Of all the poets in this study, Hayden appears to be the most successful in decentering his own ideologies. He does not abandon them, but allows himself to listen to other viewpoints, some beyond his comprehension to articulate. This inarticulation occurs when he sees myths in the sea and in the ruins of Mexico, when the cosmic seems beyond the power of human language. And, yet, it is human language that closes this sequence of poems as a unified crowd cries "Olé!" at the mysterious beauty of death and life as performed by a matador and a bull. The cruelty and the beauty of this performance mirrors Hayden's experience of Mexico. Hayden is not writing home to the United States, but appears to be writing home wherever he is. "An Inference of Mexico," a poem sequence that begins with the Day of the Dead, ends with the triumph of the living who have ritualized their parallel moments of joy and sorrow. One observation of Mexico leads into other observations of Mexico; these are inferences discovered by a curious observer rather than an individual who arrives in Mexico ready to gaze upon the country and its people through preconceived lenses.

7

Conclusion

This work, as it has unfolded over several chapters, addresses notions and issues dealing with "Americanness," by which I mean the United States as presented by the poets here. Inherent in the concept of Americanness is, of course, notions of the foreign or foreignness. "Admit that Mexico is your double ... [and] accept the doppelgänger in your psyche" (Anzaldúa 86). Mexico has always been present within our own national discourses, but it perhaps was only beginning to surface within our poetry in mainstream 1950s America. Mexico is significantly tied to notions of home. Home can be defined by location as much as by dislocation (as in the sense of foreign space). In other words, notions of home and identity are interrelated, each concept proving to be slippery and culturally defined.

By looking at Mexico through the eyes of American poets, the reader is forced to reconsider the greater world. Tourism involves "the increased fascination of the developed world with the cultural practices of less developed societies" (Urry 57); the poet's responsibility may be to investigate this fascination. Mexico and its "cultural practices," as part of the Hispanic world (which transcends borders, including U.S. borders), help construct a complicated postwar United States and its own surprisingly fluid ideas of political and cultural borders.

William Carlos Williams's brief trip into Juárez just for dinner was the impetus for his major, long poem, "The Desert Music," a polyvocal work about a very personal quest. In this work, Williams investigates his Americanness and his own ambivalence surrounding his Hispanic heritage. The transnational border crossing in "The Desert Music" awakens Williams to the potential of the desert and to the potentials buried within his Hispanic heritage. It is only on foreign soil, no matter how brief the journey, where he begins to confront the Other inside himself. Williams, in this poem, can no longer ignore the long journey toward the "Carlos" that is his middle name. In the following three chapters I turn to visits by three Beat authors: Kerouac, Corso and Ginsberg.

In Jack Kerouac's blues-chorus sequence entitled *Mexico City Blues*, Mexico has very little textual presence. The actual Mexico, as place, that would have been available to him during the writing of *Mexico City Blues* is hard to find here. Kerouac's illusions of Mexico as a place where "black and white blend and are negated by brown" (McCampbell Grace 113), a place that is more utopian than his United States, fog his vision of an actual location. Kerouac is not invested in location so much as in meditation ("his first artistic attempt to convey his Buddhist-inspired visions" [Theado 127]), geography often yielding to metaphysics throughout numerous choruses. Kerouac goes to Mexico to investigate the possible rewards to be gained through opening up his work to greater textual plurality. However, in "much of Beat writing, minorities are depicted as an enduring source of 'primitive' values whose identities remain stable and static" (Lardas 178). Kerouac, it seems, was less invested in writing Mexico than in using that country as a means of writing "America" (the United States). In his poems, Kerouac fails to see Mexicans in the context of their own contemporary, protean realities; thus, *Mexico City Blues* can be seen as a text of polyvocality, but of one whose agency for change or critique is limited in scope and success.

Gregory Corso looks at Mexico and is less than enthusiastic about the country. Basically, he makes no attempt to negotiate his views with the concept of the foreign; consequently, he ironically retreats into an American identity, at least within the confines of his two poems specifically about Mexico: "Mexican Impressions" and "Puma in Chapultepec Zoo." These poems reveal Corso's ethnocentrism; thus, what is foregrounded in these works about Mexico does not help the reader see any genuine sense of Mexico, its landscape or culture. Indeed,

7. Conclusion

Corso's failure to immerse himself in any Mexican experience foregrounds his own surprisingly provincial ideologies. Although Corso may investigate "the hollow image of American success" in other poems, his travel to Mexico fails to "[celebrate] the richness of the journey" (Lardas 170). Corso is writing about America (the United States) rather than writing about Mexico, and rather nostalgically at that, an American outsider seeing the links to fellow citizens as more important than to the Mexican as fellow proletariat.

Allen Ginsberg is committed to confronting his reactions to being "away" and dislocated. Being outside of "America" (his "metonymic relationship with America" (Lardas 90]) and problematizing what he looks at externally, as well as internally, Ginsberg invests in challenging the hegemony of the United States and examining naturalized hegemonic Americanness within himself. "Siesta in Xbalba," Ginsberg's long poem about Mexico, is an exploration of the interior self that requires a Whitmanesque accounting of the exterior world. Ginsberg projects himself beyond the topographical. His cosmic self and reflective narcissism expand his consciousness into the realm of history, which proves to be a temporal and spatial universe. Geography and the metaphysical self are juxtaposed in Ginsberg's time in Mexico; his trip into deep Mexico becomes, ultimately, a quest to find an emerging poetic voice to suit his accentuated identity. This quest is to find a cosmic voice, one equipped to perhaps reconnect America to "its natural source" (Lardas 111).

Denise Levertov is much more than a distant or meditative observer of Mexico, its culture and its history; she is on "a voyage of discovery" (Rodgers 68). Her experiences, as articulated in her poems about Mexico, accentuate acceptance and welcome of the new, the different. There is no need to fear or dismiss the foreign. Levertov's poems about Mexico open up issues of literary representation as well as notions of identity politics. For their time, Levertov's works about Mexico are quite fresh for American poetry, for in them she attempts to immerse herself in the Mexican culture in new ways, with "caring involvement" (Frenkel 30). Mexico becomes another opportunity for experiences, many of which can be transformed into texts celebrating our shared humanity.

Robert Hayden's poem sequence, "An Inference of Mexico," springs from his experiences in Mexico in the 1950s (on a Ford Foundation Fellowship). Hayden's sequence is informed by multiple voices, moments of heteroglossia, "space with other voices" (D.T. Turner 99). As a poet and observer, Hayden deliberately rejects the option to speak for Mexicans and makes the decision to have voices of the "locals" included in his work. His success on these levels may be due to multiple factors: religious affiliation, superior Spanish language skills, and his cultural status as an African American traveling through a racially diverse region of Mexico. This poem sequence complicates any simple notion of Other, especially when place becomes a primary factor shaping the literary work. Hayden embraces both location and dislocation so that being south of himself, he has views of himself in new circumstances and of others in their everyday circumstances.

In the end, the romantic gaze, the touristic gaze and the poetic gaze are concepts which intersect, overlap or altogether stand alone, depending upon multiple factors. In terms of the poets studied here, the least imperialistic gazes are those conducted by poets whose characteristics were best equipped for travel to a foreign country, in this case Mexico. Simply arriving somewhere does not ensure immersion into a culture (which some of these poets, but not all, certainly expected); immersion into a culture requires "the need to be an educated traveler" (Urry 87). Although the variety of experiences of these writers may still be typical for general contemporary travelers, global culture moves more and more toward "packaged, themed environments whereby a relatively sanitized representation of rural life is constructed and presented to visitors" (Urry 89). This sanitization will prove to have a profound impact on literature, preconceptions as walls between ourselves (and our writers) and the complex world larger than our world views. When these American poets of the 1950s arrive in "their" Mexico, they can still encounter the contradictions of being tourists and voluntary exiles, even if temporarily so. The compass, it turns out, is about so much more than the primary four directions.

Works Cited

Alarcón, Norma. "Anzaldúa's *Frontera:* Inscribing Gynetics." *Displacement, Diaspora, and Geographies of Identity.* Ed. Smadar Lavie and Ted Swedenburg. Durham: Duke University Press, 1996. pp. 41–53.
Altieri, Charles. *Enlarging the Temple.* Lewisburg, PA: Bucknell University Press, 1979.
Anzaldúa, Gloria. *Borderlands/La Frontera: The New Mestiza.* San Francisco: Spinsters/Aunt Lute, 1987.
Bakhtin, M.M. "Epic and Novel: Toward a Methodology for the Study of the Novel." *The Dialogic Imagination: Four Essays.* Ed. Michael Holquist. Austin: University of Texas Press, 1981. pp. 3–40.
_____. "From the Prehistory of Novelistic Discourse." *The Dialogic Imagination: Four Essays.* Ed. Michael Holquist. Austin: University of Texas Press, 1981. pp. 41–83.
_____. "The Problem of Speech Genres." *Speech Genres and Other Late Essays.* Ed. Caryl Emerson and Michael Holquist. Austin: University of Texas Press, 1986. pp. 60–102.
Bayón, Damián, and Murillo Marx. *History of South American Colonial Art and Architecture: Spanish South America and Brazil.* New York: Rizzoli, 1992.
Bergman, David. *Gaiety Transfigured: Gay Self-Representation in American Literature.* Madison: University of Wisconsin Press, 1991.
Berry, Jason, Jonathan Foose and Tad Jones. *Up from the Cradle of Jazz: New Orleans Music Since World War II.* Athens: University of Georgia Press, 1986.
Bersani, Leo. *Homos.* Cambridge: Harvard University Press, 1995.
Bertens, Hans. "Postmodern Culture(s)." *Postmodernism and Contemporary Fiction.* Ed. Edmund J. Smyth. London: B.T. Batsford Ltd., 1991.
Bhabha, Homi K. "DessimiNation: time, narrative, and the margins of the modern nation." *Nation and Narration.* Ed. Homi K. Bhabha. London: Routledge, 1990. pp. 291–322.

Works Cited

Boldy, Steven. "Carlos Fuentes." *On Modern Latin American Fiction*. Ed. John King. New York: Noonday Press, 1987. pp. 155–172.

Bowering, George. "Denise Levertov." *Denise Levertov: Selected Criticism*. Ed. Albert Gelpi. Ann Arbor: University of Michigan Press, 1993. pp. 243–54.

Boyd, Melba Joyce. "Poetry from Detroit's Black Bottom: The Tension between Belief and Ideology in the Work of Robert Hayden." *Robert Hayden: Essays on the Poetry*. Ed. Laurence Goldstein and Robert Chrisman. Ann Arbor: University of Michigan Press, 2001. pp. 205–215.

Bremen, Brian. "Denise Levertov." *Denise Levertov: Selected Criticism*. Ed. Albert Gelpi. Ann Arbor: University of Michigan Press, 1993. 243–54.

Breslin, James B. "The Origins of 'Howl' and 'Kaddish.'" *On the Poetry of Allen Ginsberg*. Ed. Lewis Hyde. Ann Arbor: University of Michigan Press, 1984. pp. 401–433.

Burns, Glen. *Great Poets Howl: A Study of Allen Ginsberg's Poetry, 1943–1955*. Frankfurt: Peter Lang, 1983.

Cassady, Carolyn. *Heart Beat: My Life with Jack and Neal*. Berkeley, CA: Creative Arts Books Co., 1976.

Charters, Ann. *Kerouac: A Biography*. San Francisco: Straight Arrow Books, 1973.

Christensen, Inger. *The Shadow of the Dome: Organicism and Romantic Poetry*. Bergen, Norway: University of Bergen, 1985.

Collecott, Diana Surman. "Inside and Outside in the Poetry of Denise Levertov." *Denise Levertov: Selected Criticism*. Ed. Albert Gelpi. Ann Arbor: University of Michigan Press, 1993. pp. 110–25.

Corso, Gregory. *Gasoline*. San Francisco: City Lights Books, 1958.

———. *Mindfield: New and Selected Poems*. New York: Thunder's Mouth Press, 1989.

Covarrubias, Miguel. *Mexico South: The Isthmus of Tehuantepec*. New York: Knopf, 1946.

Davis, Francis. *The History of the Blues*. New York: Hyperion, 1995.

Docherty, Brian. "Allen Ginsberg." *American Poetry: The Modernist Ideal*. Ed. Clive Bloom and Brian Docherty. New York: St. Martin's Press, 1995. pp. 199–217.

Doty, Mark. "The 'Forbidden Planet' of Character: The Revolutions of the 1950s." *A Profile of Twentieth-Century American Poetry*. Ed. Jack Myers and David Wojahn. Carbondale: Southern Illinois University Press, 1991. pp. 131–157.

Douglas, Ann. "Telepathic Shock and Meaning Excitement: Kerouac's Poetics of Intimacy." *The Beat Generation: Critical Essays*. Ed. Kostas Myrsiades. New York: Peter Lang, 2002. pp. 21–36.

Eberhart, Richard. "West Coast Rhythms." *On the Poetry of Allen Ginsberg*. Ed. Lewis Hyde. Ann Arbor: University of Michigan Press, 1984. pp. 24–25.

Elliott, Michael. *The Day Before Yesterday*. New York: Simon & Schuster, 1996.

Emanuel, James A. "On *Selected Poems*." *Robert Hayden: Essays on the Poetry*. Ed.

Laurence Goldstein and Robert Chrisman. Ann Arbor: University of Michigan Press, 2001. pp. 63–64.

Fetrow, Fred M. *Robert Hayden*. Boston: Twayne, 1984.

Fisher-Wirth, Ann W. *William Carlos Williams and Autobiography: The Woods of His Own Nature*. University Park: Pennsylvania State University Press, 1989.

Foster, Edward Halsey. *Understanding the Beats*. Columbia: University of S. Carolina Press, 1992.

French, Warren. *Jack Kerouac*. Boston: Twayne, 1986.

Frenkel, Harris. "Denise Levertov and the Lyric of the Contingent Self." *Denise Levertov: New Perspectives*. Ed. Anne Colclough Little and Susie Paul. Locust Hill Literary Studies Series 28. West Cornwall, CT: Locust Hill Press, 2000. pp. 17–34.

Gibbons, Reginald. "A Man That in His Writing Was Most Wise." *Robert Hayden: Essays on the Poetry*. Ed. Laurence Goldstein and Robert Chrisman. Ann Arbor: University of Michigan Press, 2001. pp. 216–222.

Gifford, Barry, and Lawrence Lee. *Jack's Book: An Oral Biography of Jack Kerouac*. New York: St. Martin's Press, 1978.

Ginsberg, Allen. *As Ever: The Collected Correspondence of Allen Ginsberg and Neal Cassady*. Ed. Barry Gifford. Berkeley: Creative Arts Book Co. 1977.

_____. *Collected Poems 1947–1980*. Cambridge: Harper & Row, 1984.

_____. "Improvised Poetics." *Composed on the Tongue*. Ed. Donald Hall. Bolinas CA: Grey Fox Press, 1980. pp. 18–62.

_____. Introduction. *Gasoline*. By Gregory Corso. San Francisco: City Lights Books, 1958. pp. 7–8.

_____. *Journals: Early Fifties Early Sixties*. Ed. Gordon Hall. New York: Grove Press, 1977.

_____. "Notes Written on Finally Finishing 'Howl.'" *On the Poetry of Allen Ginsberg*. Ed. Lewis Hyde. Ann Arbor: University of Michigan Press, 1984. pp. 180–83.

Gish, Nancy K. "Denise Levertov." *American Poetry: The Modernist Ideal*. Ed. Clive Bloom and Brian Docherty. New York: St. Martin's Press, 1995. pp. 253–70.

Gitzen, Julian. "From Reverence to Attention: The Poetry of Denise Levertov." *Critical Essays on Denise Levertov*. Ed. Linda Wagner-Martin. Boston: Hall & Co., 1991. pp. 123–32.

Goldstein, Laurence, and Robert Chrisman. "Introduction." *Robert Hayden: Essays on the Poetry*. Ed. Laurence Goldstein and Robert Chrisman. Ann Arbor: University of Michigan Press, 2001. pp. 1–5.

González Echevarría, Roberto. *Alejo Carpentier: The Pilgrim at Home*. Ithaca, NY: Cornell University Press, 1977.

Guimarães Rosa, João. "The Third Bank of the River." *Contemporary Latin American Short Stories*. Ed. Pat McNees. New York: Fawcett Columbine, 1996. pp. 147–52.

Works Cited

Gunn, Drewey Wayne. *American and British Writers in Mexico, 1556–1973*. 1969. Austin: University of Texas Press, 1974.

Gutiérrez Brockington, Lolita. *The Leverage of Labor: Managing the Cortés Haciendas in Tehuantepec, 1588–1688*. Durham, NC Duke University Press, 1989.

Halberstam, David. *The Fifties*. New York: Villard Books, 1993.

Hanson, Katherine, and Ed Block. "Gender, Nature, and Spirit: Justifying Female Complexity in the Later Poetry of Denise Levertov." *Denise Levertov: New Perspectives*. Ed. Anne Colclough Little and Susie Paul. Locust Hill Literary Studies Series 28. West Cornwall, CT: Locust Hill Press, 2000. pp. 63–76.

Harper, Michael S. "Angles of Ascent." *Robert Hayden: Essays on the Poetry*. Ed. Laurence Goldstein and Robert Chrisman. Ann Arbor: University of Michigan Press, 2001. 74–77.

Hatcher, John S. *From the Auroral Darkness: The Life and Poetry of Robert Hayden*. Oxford: George Ronald, 1984.

Hayden, Robert. *Collected Poems*. New York: Liveright Publishing Corp., 1985.

———. "A Conversation with A. Poulin Jr." *Robert Hayden: Essays on the Poetry*. Ed. Laurence Goldstein and Robert Chrisman. Ann Arbor: University of Michigan Press, 2001. pp. 30–40.

Hipkiss, Robert A. *Jack Kerouac: Prophet of the New Romanticism*. Lawrence: Regents Press of Kansas, 1976.

Hirsch, Edward. "Mean to Be Free." *Robert Hayden: Essays on the Poetry*. Ed. Laurence Goldstein and Robert Chrisman. Ann Arbor: University of Michigan Press, 2001. pp. 80–84.

Hunt, Tim. *Kerouac's Crooked Road: Development of a Fiction*. Hamden CT: Archon Books, 1981.

Jackson, Richard. *The Dismantling of Time in Contemporary Poetry*. Tuscaloosa: University of Alabama Press, 1988.

Jones, James T. *A Map of Mexico City Blues: Jack Kerouac as Poet*. Carbondale: Southern Illinois University Press, 1992.

Juhasz, Suzanne. "'The Enactment of Rites': The Poetry of Denise Levertov." *Naked and Fiery Forms: Modern American Poetry by Women, A New Tradition*. New York: Harper Colophon, 1976. pp. 57–84.

Kaplan, Caren. *Questions of Travel: Postmodern Discourses of Displacement*. Durham, NC: Duke University Press, 1996.

Kerouac, Jack. "The First Word." *Kerouac's Last Word: Jack Kerouac in Escapade*. Ed. Tom Clark. Sudbury, MA: Water Row Press, 1986. pp. 45–49.

———. *Mexico City Blues: 242 Choruses*. New York: Grove, 1959.

———. "Mexico Fellaheen." *Lonesome Traveller*. New York: Ballantine, 1960. pp. 21–36.

———. *Selected Letters 1940–1956*. Ed. Ann Charters. New York: Viking, 1995.

Kinnahan, Linda A. *Poetics of the Feminine: Authority and Literary Tradition in William Carlos Williams, Mina Loy, Denise Levertov, and Kathleen Fraser*. New York: Cambridge University Press, 1994.

Works Cited

Kouidis, Virginia. "Denise Levertov: Her Illustrious Ancestry." *Critical Essays on Denise Levertov.* Ed. Linda Wagner-Martin. Boston: Hall & Co., 1991. pp. 254–72.

Lardas, John. "Holy the Bop Apocalypse!: A Religious Interpretation of Beat Poetics and Style." Master's thesis. Miami University, 1996.

Levertov, Denise. *Collected Earlier Poems 1940–1960.* New York: New Directions, 1979.

———. "Dying and Living." *Denise Levertov: In Her Own Province.* Insights II: Working Papers in Contemporary Criticism. Ed. Linda Wagner. New York: New Directions, 1979. pp. 49–59.

———. "Interweavings: Reflections on the Role of Dream in the Making of Poems." *Light Up the Cave.* New York: New Directions, 1981. pp. 29–45.

———. *New York Quarterly* Craft Interview." *Denise Levertov: In Her Own Province.* Insights II: Working Papers in Contemporary Criticism. Ed. Linda Welshimer Wagner. New York: New Directions, 1979 pp. 1–21.

———. "The Sense of Pilgrimage." *The Poet in the World.* New York: New Directions, 1973. 62–86.

———. "Williams and the Duende." *New and Selected Essays.* New York: New Directions, 1992. pp. 33–43.

———. "Williams and Eliot." *New and Selected Essays.* New York: New Directions, 1992. pp. 59–66.

Lhamon W.T., Jr. *Deliberate Speed: The Origins of a Cultural Style in the American 1950s.* Washington, D.C.: Smithsonian Institution Press, 1990.

Lomnitz-Adler, Claudio. *Exits from the Labyrinth: Culture and Ideology in the Mexican National Space.* Berkeley: University of California Press, 1992.

Malkoff, Karl. *Crowell's Handbook of Contemporary American Poetry.* New York: Crowell Co., 1973.

Mariani, Paul. "'The Desert Music.'" *Critical Essays on William Carlos Williams.* Critical Essays on American Literature. Ed. Steven Gould Axelrod and Helen Deese. New York: Hall & Co., 1995. pp. 124–28.

Marten, Harry. *Understanding Denise Levertov.* Columbia: University of S. Carolina Press, 1988.

Martin, Emily. "Body Narratives, Body Boundaries." *Cultural Studies.* Ed. Lawrence Grossberg, Cary Nelson and Paula A. Treichler. New York: Routledge, 1992. pp. 409–23.

Marzán, Julio. *The Spanish American Roots of William Carlos Williams.* Austin: University of Texas Press, 1994.

McCampbell Grace, Nancy. "A White Man in Love: A Study of Race, Gender, Class, and Ethnicity in Jack Kerouac's *Maggie Cassidy, The Subterraneans* and *Trestessa. The Beat Generation Critical Essays.* Ed. Kosta Myrsiades. New York: Peter Lang, 2002. pp. 93–120.

Merrill, Thomas F. *Allen Ginsberg.* Boston: Twayne, 1988.

Miles, Barry. *Ginsberg: A Biography.* New York: Simon & Schuster, 1989.

Miller, J. Hillis. *Topographies.* Stanford, CA: Stanford University Press, 1995.

Works Cited

Moramarco, Fred. "Moloch's Poet." *On the Poetry of Allen Ginsberg*. Ed. Lewis Hyde. Ann Arbor: University of Michigan Press, 1984. pp. 222–30.

Mullen, Harryette, and Stephen Yenser. "Theme and Variations on Robert Hayden's Poetry." *Robert Hayden: Essays on the Poetry*. Ed. Laurence Goldstein and Robert Chrisman. Ann Arbor: University of Michigan Press, 2001. pp. 233–247.

Nicosia, Gerald. *Memory Babe: A Critical Biography of Jack Kerouac*. New York: Penguin, 1985.

Olson, Kirby. *Gregory Corso: Doubting Thomist*. Carbondale: Southern Illinois University Press, 2002.

Pacernick, Gary. "Interview with Denise Levertov." *Denise Levertov: New Perspectives*. Ed. Anne Colclough Little and Susie Paul. Locust Hill Literary Studies Series 28. West Cornwall, CT: Locust Hill Press, 2000. pp. 85–92.

Panish, Jon. "Kerouac's *The Subterraneans*." *MELUS* 19:3 (1994): 107–23.

Paul, Sherman. *The Music of Survival: A Biography of a Poem by William Carlos Williams*. Urbana: University of Illinois Press, 1968.

Powell, Michael. "The Locomotive Poetic of Jack Kerouac's *Mexico City Blues*." *Notes of Modern American Literature* 9:2 (1985): item 8.

Rando, Therese A. "Death and Dying Are Not and Should Not Be Taboo Topics." *Principles of Thanatology*. Ed. A.H. Kutscher, A.C. Carr and L.G. Kutscher. New York: Columbia University Press, 1987. pp. 31–65.

Robinson, Cecil. *With the Ears of Strangers: The Mexican in American Literature*. Tucson: University of Arizona Press, 1963.

Rodgers, Audrey T. *Denise Levertov: The Poetry of Engagement*. Rutherford, NJ: Fairleigh Dickinson University Press, 1993.

Schumacher, Michael. *Dharma Lion: A Critical Biography of Allen Ginsberg*. New York: St. Martin's Press, 1992.

Skau, Michael. *"A Clown in a Grave": Complexities and Tensions in the Works of Gregory Corso*. Carbondale: Southern Illinois University Press, 1999.

Snodgrass, W.D. "Robert Hayden: The Man in the Middle." *Robert Hayden: Essays on the Poetry*. Ed. Laurence Goldstein and Robert Chrisman. Ann Arbor: University of Michigan Press, 2001. pp. 223–232.

Stephenson, Gregory. "'The Arcadian Map': Notes on the Poetry of Gregory Corso." *The Daybreak Boys: Essays on the Literature of the Beat Generation*. Carbondale: Southern Illinois University Press, pp. 74–89.

_____. *Exiled Angel: A Study of the Work of Gregory Corso*. London: Hearing Eye, 1989.

Swartz, Omar. *The View from On the Road*. Carbondale: Southern Illinois University Press, 1999.

Theado, Mark. *Understanding Jack Kerouac*. Columbia: University of South Carolina Press, 2000.

Torgovnick, Marianna. *Gone Primitive: Savage Intellects, Modern Lives*. Chicago: University of Chicago Press, 1990.

Works Cited

Turner, Darwin T. "Robert Hayden Remembered." *Robert Hayden: Essays on the Poetry.* Ed. Laurence Goldstein and Robert Chrisman. Ann Arbor: University of Michigan Press, 2001. pp. 87–103.

Turner, Steve. *Angelheaded Hipster: A Life of Jack Kerouac.* New York: Viking, 1996.

Tytell, John. *Naked Angels: The Lives and Literature of the Beat Generation.* New York: Grove Press, 1976.

Ullman, Leslie. "American Poetry in the 1960s." *A Profile of Twentieth-Century American Poetry.* Ed. Jack Myers and David Wojahn. Carbondale: Southern Illinois University Press, 1991. pp. 190–223.

Urry, John. *The Tourist Gaze.* Theory, Culture and Society. 1990. London: Sage Publications, 2002.

von Hallberg, Robert. *Charles Olson: The Scholar's Act.* Cambridge University Press, 1978.

Wagner-Martin, Linda. "Levertov: Poetry and the Spiritual." *Critical Essays on Denise Levertov.* Ed. Linda Wagner-Martin. Boston: Hall & Co., 1991. pp. 196–204.

Walter, Tony. *The Revival of Death.* London: Routledge, 1994.

Weinreich, Regina. *The Spontaneous Poetics of Jack Kerouac: A Study of the Fiction.* Carbondale: Southern Illinois University Press, 1987.

What Happened to Jack Kerouac? Richard Lerner Productions. Videocassette. Vidmark, 1985.

Williams, Pontheolla T. *Robert Hayden: A Critical Analysis of His Poetry.* Urbana: University of Illinois Press, 1987.

Williams, William Carlos. *The Autobiography of William Carlos Williams.* New York: Random House, 1951.

_____. *The Collected Poems of William Carlos Williams, Volume II: 1939–1962.* New York: New Directions, 1962.

Williams Wilburn, Jr. "Covenant of Timelessness and Time: Symbolism and History in Robert Hayden's *Angle of Ascent*." *Robert Hayden: Essays on the Poetry.* Ed. Laurence Goldstein and Robert Chrisman. Ann Arbor: University of Michigan Press, 2001. pp. 155–174.

Wilson, Steve. "The Author as Spiritual Pilgrim: The Search for Authenticity in Jack Kerouac's *On the Road* and *The Subterraneans*." *The Beat Generation: Critical Essays.* Ed. Kostas Myrsiades. New York: Peter Lang, 2002. pp. 77–91.

Younoszai, Barbara. "Mexican American Perspectives Related to Death." *Ethnic Variations in Dying, Death, and Grief: Diversity in Universality.* Washington, DC: Taylor and Francis, 1993. pp. 67–78.

Index

Africa 40, 150
African-American heritage 8–9, 34, 36–37, 43, 52, 61, 63, 64, 148, 150, 154, 161, 163, 178
Al Que Quiere 18, 20
Andalusia 27
Anti-Semitism 94
Anzaldúa, Gloria 11
Arabia 111
Arcadia 72
"The Artist" 142, 144
As Ever 96, 115, 118
Australia 40
The Autobiography 18 20
Aztec culture 42–43, 47, 51–52, 54, 58, 166, 167, 172

Babel 80
Bahá'í religion 149–50, 155, 163, 170, 178
Ballad of Remembrance 147, 154
The Beats 5 7, 33, 34, 36, 37, 38, 45–46, 56, 58, 61, 67, 69, 81, 88, 89, 96, 101, 108, 117, 121, 122, 143, 176
Beethoven, Ludwig van 52
Berkeley (CA) 6
Blake, William 103
Bontemps, Arna 147
British heritage 8
"Broken Glass" 128
Buddhism 32, 39–40, 42, 49–50, 59, 60, 61, 176
Burroughs, William 81

California 118
Carpentier, Alejo 50
Casals, Pablo 20–21
Cassady, Carolyn 42, 54, 56
Cassady, Neal 35, 64, 121
Castañeda, Carlos 40
Catholicism 39, 49, 59, 167
Central Park 127
"Central Park, Winter, after Sunset" 127–28, 141
Chapultepec Zoo 83–84
Chiapas 91, 93, 96, 99, 102, 118, 119, 120, 151
Chichén Itzá 104
Christianity 39, 109, 141, 150, 169, 170, 172
Civil Rights Movement 37
Coatlicue 166–67
Columbus, Christopher 78
Confessionalism 94
Corso, Gregory 1, 4, 5, 7, 67–89, 93, 123, 176–77
Crane, Hart 17
Cuba 91

Day of the Dead/*El Día de los Muertos* 151–53, 154–63, 173
Death Valley 41
"The Desert Music" 1, 6, 13–29, 151, 175–76
Dionysian presence 27
Duncan, Robert 120–21

Index

Eastern spirituality 32
Eden 118, 140–41
Eisenhower, Dwight D. 63
El Paso (TX) 10, 14, 16–17, 20
Eliot, T.S. 17, 108
Empty Mirror 103
English literary tradition 124
Euro-American heritage 56, 133–34
Europe 10, 26, 47, 111, 112, 124, 150, 154
European genealogy 76

Fellaheen 39, 41, 43, 56
"The First Word" 44
"Five Poems from Mexico" 124
Ford Foundation Fellowship 147, 178
Foucault, Michel 61
French-Canadian heritage and language 7, 34–36, 40, 45, 47–48, 51, 52, 60, 64

Garver, Bill 81
Gasoline 7, 69, 73
Ginsberg, Allen 2, 4, 5, 6, 7, 68, 69, 88, 91–122, 123, 146, 176, 177
Goodman, Mitchell 7, 69, 123
Grand Prix de la Poésie 147
Great Britain 123, 125, 135
Guadalajara 69, 123
Guanajuato 115–16
Guatemala 91
Guaymas 72, 75

Harlem (NYC, NY) 100 112
Hayden, Robert 2, 5, 8, 58, 123, 147–173, 178; biological mother of 9
Hayden, William, and Sue Ellen 9
Heaven and Other Poems 31
Here and Now 127, 128, 133
Hispanic/Latino heritage 4, 13, 15, 18, 19, 25, 26, 29, 175–76
Holland 127, 128
"Howl" 112
Howl and Other Poems 117
Hughes, Langston 147
Ignorino 57

Indian heritage 19, 40, 46, 48, 55, 61, 71, 75, 80, 95, 96, 109–10, 150
"An Inference of Mexico" 2, 9, 147–73, 178
Instituto Geologica 111
"Islands" 156
Italian-American heritage 68

The Jacob's Ladder 124
Jalisco 129
Java 127, 128
Jolson, Al 51, 52
Juárez 6, 13, 16–18, 20–21, 23–25, 27, 173
Juchitán 153, 157–58
Judaism and Jews 51, 52, 92, 113, 143, 154

Keats, John 160
Kerouac, Jack 1, 4, 5, 6, 31–65, 81, 88, 93, 121, 123, 149, 176; mother of 39
Kierkegaard, Søren Aabye 57
"Kodachromes of the Island" 156

"The Lagoon" 128
Latin American heritage 14
Le Maitre, Yvonne 34
Levertov, Denise 2, 5, 7, 8, 14, 58, 69, 123–146, 177
Lowell (MA) 35, 39, 62

Manichean heresy 25
Marauding Marade 57
Marxism 56
Mayan culture 91, 97, 103, 104, 105, 113, 119, 120
McAlmon, Robert 6, 14
Merton, Thomas 27
Mexicali 118
Mexican Americans 37, 48, 64
"Mexican Impressions" 1–2, 67–89, 176
Mexico City 31–65, 81
Mexico City Blues 1, 6, 31–65, 149, 176; "3rd Chorus" 45, 55; "5th Chorus" 46; "9th Chorus" 41, 46; "12th Chorus" 1, 47–50; "13th Chorus" 42–44; "14th Chorus" 42–44; "36th Cho-

rus" 50; "103rd Chorus" 55; "116th Chorus" 1, 50–52; "119th Chorus" 43; "124th Chorus" 59; "134th Chorus" 1, 50, 52, 55; "137th Chorus" 43; "197th Chorus" 59; "222nd Chorus" 1, 50, 54, 59; "242nd Chorus" 59–60
"Mexico Fellaheen" 37, 44
Miles, Davis 51, 52
Minor Characters 121
Mississippi River 44
Moloch 94, 112, 120
Moriarty, Dean 65

New England 48
New Orleans (LA) 41
New Testament 119
New York (NY) 62, 68, 83, 84, 86–87, 96, 98–101, 106, 111, 118, 120, 123, 127, 128
"Notes Written on Finally Recording 'Howl'" 109

Oaxaca 150, 151
O'Hara, Frank 121
On the Road 6, 38, 39, 40, 65
Orizaba Street 55, 57, 81
Orlovsky, Peter 69
"Overland to the Islands" 2, 124, 127, 128, 133–36, 138
Overland to the Islands 128, 133

Palenque 91, 96, 99, 100, 122
"The Palm Tree" 128
Parker, Charlie 52, 59
Paterson 22, 23
Paterson (NJ) 23
Paz, Octavio 166
"Pleasures" 128
Pomes All Sizes 31
Popocatapetl 42
Portugal 40
Portuguese heritage 4
Poulin, A., Jr. 166
Pre-Columbian civilizations 106, 144
Puerto Rican heritage 6, 13, 19, 20, 21, 26, 83–84, 86, 151

"Puma in Chapulepec Zoo" 2 67–89, 176
"Pure Products" 128

Rilke, Rainer Maria 25
Rio Grande 24
Russians 53

San Francisco (CA) 62, 120
San Francisco poetry renaissance 6, 79
San Luis Potosí 14
San Luis Rio Colorado 72
"Scenes from the Life of the Peppertrees" 2, 124, 128, 137, 139–41
"The Sense of Pilgrimage" 144
Sheffey, Asa (Hayden's biological father) 9
Shields, Karena 91, 121–22
Sierra Madres 82, 88
"Siesta in Xbalba AND Return to the States" 2, 7, 91–122, 146, 177
Spanish heritage and language 4, 19–20, 24, 27, 32, 36, 44–46, 53, 55, 61, 138, 142, 147, 148, 149–50, 163, 168, 178
Stevens, Wallace 129
"Sunday Afternoon" 128
"A Supermarket in Guadalajara, Mexico" 2, 124, 128, 136–39

Tehuacán 167
Tehuantepec 151–52, 152, 157, 158
Tehuantepec, Gulf of 151
Tehuantepec Isthmus 150, 151, 152
Teotihuacan 43–44
Thoreau, Henry David 135
Toltec 142, 166
Tomatlan 129
"Tomatlan (Variations)" 2, 124, 126, 128, 129–32
The Town and the City 34
"Triple Feature" 2, 124, 128, 142–44
Tristessa 62
Tristessa 39

Index

Veracruz 165–66

Washington (DC) 41
Western Hemisphere 111
"The Whirlwind" 128
Whitman, Walt 95, 108, 119, 121
Whitmanesque 17, 42, 93, 108, 109, 116
Williams, Flossie 14, 28
Williams, William Carlos 1, 3, 5, 6, 8, 13–29, 123, 141, 151, 175–76

With Eyes at the Back of Our Heads 124, 128, 141, 142, 144
World War II 14, 46, 69

Xibalba (Xbalba) 96–97, 99, 103
"Xochipilli" 2 124, 128, 142, 144–46
Xochipilli 144, 146

Yucatán peninsula 96, 107, 152

Zoroastrian dualism 25

www.ingramcontent.com/pod-product-compliance
Lightning Source LLC
Chambersburg PA
CBHW032101300426

44116CB00007B/848